John Sinclair

Scenes and Stories of the North of Scotland

John Sinclair

Scenes and Stories of the North of Scotland

ISBN/EAN: 9783337006983

Printed in Europe, USA, Canada, Australia, Japan

Cover: Foto ©Thomas Meinert / pixelio.de

More available books at **www.hansebooks.com**

SCENES AND STORIES

OF THE

NORTH OF SCOTLAND.

From Photo. by G. W. Wilson.

EILAN-DONAN CASTLE, LOCHALSH, ROSS-SHIRE.

SCENES AND STORIES

OF THE

NORTH OF SCOTLAND.

BY

JOHN SINCLAIR,

AUTHOR OF "HEATHER BELLES," ETC., ETC.

WITH THREE COLOURED AND EIGHT LITHOGRAPH ILLUSTRATIONS.

EDINBURGH: JAMES THIN.
LONDON: SIMPKIN MARSHALL & CO.
1890.

PREFACE.

THIS book has been written with a three-fold aim : to awaken interest, to stimulate, and to amuse.

The scenes described have been selected chiefly from parts of Scotland which are remote, or aside, from the ordinary thoroughfares of travel, and are therefore less known than they deserve to be. I have tried to present them as vividly as possible, so as to awaken in others an interest in them. If many more travellers are induced to visit these localities, they will not be disappointed, and I shall be pleased.

Again, no one reaps full benefit from travel who does not go to and fro with open eyes, open ears, open mind, and open heart. What a pitiful lot are many of our modern sight "do"-ers, who take in no more from nature than the eye of a calf might do ! Not for these do I write ; but for very many—I hope the majority after all—who long to taste the sweet secrets of nature, and through these to reach a better knowledge of her great Author. I like to think that God, Who has made all that is beautiful and grand, and has given to us any sense or love of these which we possess, is Himself the prime Admirer of the varied scenery of His world. My aim has been that these pages should feed the love of nature, and stimulate the study of her works with that all-round " openness " which I have commended above.

As for the incidents and stories scattered here and there, they have been inserted simply to interest and amuse. Not even a wild Highland landscape is perfect without its little curl of smoke in a corner to suggest some relation between nature and mankind. Thus are one or two harmless adventures and brief sketches of character thrown in to play the part of the light blue pennant from the shepherd's cottage. I make bold to claim that these incidents and anecdotes, with one or two trifling exceptions, are new and fresh, in the sense that they are only known to very limited circles, and have never, so far as I am aware, appeared in print.

If these "Scenes and Stories" prove acceptable to the public, the Author has material enough to form the basis of another series, still drawn from his native Scotland.

JOHN SINCLAIR.

July 1890.

CONTENTS.

LIST OF ILLUSTRATIONS.

SCUIR-OURAN AND SCUIR-NA-CARNICH, LOCH DUICH.

SCENES AND STORIES.

CHAPTER I.

LOCH DUICH, ROSS-SHIRE.

It may not perhaps be wise to begin my book by rubbing the fur of some readers the wrong way, but justice to my subject and to my own intense convictions leave me no choice.

Do you know Loch Duich? Hundreds answer, Yes. Then I am sure you will bid others listen while I tell my story. On the other hand, thousands upon thousands answer, No. Then you have not yet seen a Scottish sea-loch, which, for interest and attractiveness, has few rivals; some would even say, no equal. Allow me a word or two with the hundreds. They very promptly answered, Yes; but I am doubtful of some of them. Will you kindly step into the witness box, one of you, please? Thank you. Now, sir, you say you know Loch Duich? Yes. Have you sailed up its waters? No, I have not. Have you walked around its shores? No, not exactly. Have you ever spent a night within hearing of its ripple? I cannot say I have. Have you ever seen the Five Sisters of Kintail? No; who or what are they? So ho! you, sir, have turned questioner now; please don't ask me in the meantime; I shall introduce

A

you to the ladies by-and-bye. Before you leave the box, will you allow me to guess the history and amount of your knowledge of Loch Duich? You were going north or coming south by one of Mr Macbrayne's excellent fleet of steamers. She came up Loch Alsh, and swung round for perhaps twenty minutes off a small pier called Totaig. There you were almost in Loch Duich, but not quite. It is as if you leant your shoulder against the right-hand door-post, and then told me you knew the house. The claim is absurd; and as you have confessed never to have seen the inmates—who are never away from home—you may go down. So the process of cross-examination might go on with one and another and another; and in the end not more than five out of each hundred would be found, in any worthy sense, to know Loch Duich.

My first acquaintance with Loch Duich began like that of the witness above. We had come—pardon me, that "we" is not editorial, but denotes a small family party —we had come from a fortnight's pleasant sojourn in the Island of Lewis. We landed at Totaig to seek for quarters somewhere about Loch Duich, but could hear of none in the immediate neighbourhood. Leaving the others to cross by boat to Dornie, where we knew there was an inn, I travelled round the Loch on foot, inquiring for rooms at every likely door. Heavy rain fell incessantly all the day long, but I could afford to despise both the distance and the drenching, when, on reaching Dornie at night, I could report that my search had been successful. These weary seventeen miles, under West Coast rain—

quite a peculiar and powerful variety of the genus—
were my first introduction to Loch Duich ; but we all
know in ordinary life that friends do not see the best
of each other on first acquaintance.

Loch Alsh, on the west coast of Ross-shire, is a fine
broad sheet of water, the access to which from seaward is
all but closed by a rugged projecting knee of the Isle of
Skye. Only narrow channels or straits remain—Kyle
Akin on the north, and Kyle Rhea on the south—by
which vessels may creep through between the mainland
and the island. Within and between these channels lies
Loch Alsh, which at its inner end is split in two by the
mountains of Kintail, and forms Loch Long or Luing to
the north, and Loch Duich to the south, like the fore-
finger and thumb of the left hand. The former creeps
up a narrow twisted glen, at the head of which it re-
ceives from the Elchaig the brown waters which have
roared and foamed over the famous falls of Glomak. It
has, however, no special charms of its own ; so leaving
its shores at the cleavage point of Dornie, we turn our
thoughts and steps to Loch Duich. Even at the risk of
bleeding my fingers among the thorns of Celtic etymology, I may venture to record that the name seems
derived from St Duthee or Duthus, of whose history and
labours but little is known. This at least is certain, that
a church dedicated to him—an interesting specimen of
old Gothic, but now long disused—may be seen in Tain ;
while a still older chapel—now entirely ruined—stood
on a sandy eminence near the same town.

Close by the entrance of Loch Duich, on the Dornie

side, lies the low rocky islet which is crowned by the picturesque ruins of Eilandonan Castle. Seen from the water, they appear to stand just above the beach, but looked at from the shore itself, they stand out, lofty and grim, against the hills of Skye. The main portion of the building was a square keep eighty feet high, with various courts, wings, and archways on either hand. On the sloping bank nearest to the shore of the mainland, a well of clear-springing water was shielded by masonry, and high walls flanked the path between it and the keep. As at present seen, the walls are shattered and crumbling away; the turrets show many a gap and rent which the friendly ivy tries in vain to hide; the lintels and archways are broken and jagged; yet if human words and deeds were stored up in the stones which first rang with them, what romances and tragedies lie around us and at our very feet! Its defenders and assailants at many a stormy epoch were men who acted in the spirit of the chief's famous grace at meat, "Lord, turn the world upside down, that Christians may make bread of it." A castle stood here, it is said, as early as the days of Alexander II.; and for generations Eilandonan was the favourite stronghold of the mighty Mackenzies.

One of the first constables of the Castle was a Kenneth Matheson. He was succeeded by Colin Fitzgerald, an Irishman, who obtained the post as a reward for services to the king at the battle of Largs, and who married Matheson's daughter. Their son was called Kenneth after his grandfather, and his sons and descendants bore the name of Mackennich, now Mackenzie, that is, the sons of

Kenneth. So runs the story of the origin of the great clan whose chiefs were lords of Eilandonan. How far it is true, I shall not pretend to say, for in these matters it is the part of a wise man neither to be a dogmatist who is sure of everything, nor a sceptic who believes in nothing. The same caution is no less needful in respect to the abundant stories and traditions—many of them very interesting and romantic—which cling like ivy round old-world walls such as those of Eilandonan. As a tasting of these stories, true in the main, but, like snowballs, losing nothing as they go, I select one or two out of many.

Between the Macdonalds of Sleat in Skye and the Mackenzies of Eilandonan there existed a chronic feud, which burst out ever and anon into wild fury and fierce fight. As a clansman once said, "There was good mischief in those days," for slaughter and plunder were scarcely considered sinful at all. On one occasion, in 1537, when the Mackenzies were absent on some raid or expedition, the Macdonalds, with their chief at their head, sailed from Skye to Eilandonan, hoping to make it, in the absence of its defenders, an easy prey. Only the governor, Gilchrist Macrae, and his son Duncan, were in the keep. The Macdonalds landed undisturbed, and for a time scattered here and there over the grass-covered rocks. Then they approached the walls, and demanded the surrender of the garrison. Macrae and his son had no intentions in that direction. Their only reply was a shot from young Duncan's bow, and the barbed arrow sunk deep in the heel of the Chief of the Islesmen. It was the old case of Achilles over again. As the blood

gushed from the wound, Macdonald fainted, and his
devoted clansmen, alarmed for his life, lifted him up and
bore him away to his barge to carry him home to Skye.
He never reached it alive, for his followers were compelled to land him on a little island by the way; and
there he died.   Of course the Macdonalds vowed eternal
vengeance, and we are not surprised to know that this
was not their last visit to Eilandonan.   Of every man
of them for a generation it might be said :

> " For this he still lives on, careless of all
> The wreaths that glory on his path lets fall ;
> For this alone exists,—like lightning fire,
> To speed one bolt of vengeance, and expire."

On another occasion, nearly a century later, the Mackenzies had a deadly quarrel with the Macdonells of
Glengarry, whose young Chief, with a large body of men,
harried and wasted the whole district between Loch
Carron and Kintail.   As in the former case, the Chief of
the Mackenzies was absent, having gone to Mull in search
of allies, but his brave lady was equal to the occasion.
When fugitives from the ravaged district came to Eilandonan, she armed a chosen body of the clansmen, supplied
them with ammunition, and put two small cannon on
board their boats.   So equipped, the little expedition was
sent out to attempt a surprise attack upon Glengarry and
his men, who were expected to come through the Kyles
between the mainland and Skye.   The Mackenzies lay in
wait behind a small rock in the middle of the fairway.   A
cloudy sky and a blinding snow shower perfected their
ambush.   At length, young Macdonell's barge came in

sight some distance in advance of the others, and so soon
as it came abreast of them, the Mackenzies poured upon
it a heavy and ruthless fire. In the panic and confusion
which ensued, the Glengarry chief and every one of his
men were either drowned or slain. The lady of Eilandonan was a proud woman that night, and lost no time in
sending the news of victory to the absent chief. These
were days in which strategy and brute courage were
valued far above all other manly accomplishments.
Many of the clansmen were fully worthy of the epitaph
bestowed on one of their number who lies in a graveyard not far from Cape Wrath :

"Donald M'Murrough here lies low,
Ill to his friend, waur (*worse*) to his foe ;
True to his master in weird (*fate*) and woe."

Yet again, in 1531, Randolph, Earl of Murray, who had
been appointed Warden of Scotland, came to Eilandonan
to execute justice upon the Mackenzies because of some
lawless outrage. He beheaded no fewer than fifty of the
offenders, and hung out their heads to bleach on the
battlements of the castle.   Again and again, in later
days, Eilandonan passed through the ruthless vicissitudes
of war, and siege, and fire, but remained in a habitable
condition till 1719.   In that year a petty rebellion
against the crown took place, in which the Mackenzies
had the aid of a body of Spaniards.   A battle was
fought in Glenshiel, in which the royalist troops were
victorious; and soon after, Eilandonan was battered into
a ruin by a ship of war, so that traitors might have one

haunt the less in which to plot mischief against the king and the laws.

Once within the heights which guard the entrance to Loch Duich, over what an attractive scene does the eye range! Before us lies a fair stretch of green glassy water, not more than a mile broad on this hand and on that—and some six miles long straight in front, to where the further strand is crowned with mingled crags and foliage. On the west, from a long waving ridge clear-cut against the sky, steep slopes of dark green fall downward like the sides of a tent, and terminate near the water's edge in a rich fringe of trees and shrubbery. The eastern side is more rugged and varied. There we find, first a succession of rocky cliffs half covered with trees, which creep far up the mountains behind ; then sloping banks, at one part subdued into rich fields, at another clothed with waving woods ; and at length, a rounded knoll, capped with foliage, which pushes itself forward as headland, where a spur of the loch bends abruptly inward toward the valley of the Croe.

So much have we seen of the western and eastern sides of the loch, which run in almost parallel lines along its shores ; it remains to speak of its southern end, where wood and water, mountain and mist, combine to produce its charms. The inner reaches of Loch Duich are girded and guarded round by precipitous rocky ridges, which mount upward and upward until they terminate in clusters of giant peaks, a number of which are not less than three thousand feet high. Of these great mountain summits, five stand closely together

behind the head of Loch Duich, and are known as the
Five Sisters of Kintail. Behind them again, but not
visible from the shores of the loch, is Ben Attow, loftier
than them all, sitting like a proud mother with her
daughters gathered around her. Perhaps nowhere in
Scotland, except in Skye alone, are so many Alpine Bens
crowded into so small a circle, as those which watch
over Glenshiel and Glen Lichd, as they slope downward
to meet in Loch Duich.

It would be rash for one who has, as the Celts say,
"only one side to his tongue," to attempt either to
spell, or, if he could spell, to pronounce the names of
the Five Sisters of Kintail. Let them remain a sacred
mystery, "nameless by day," like the secret title of
the Clan Macgregor, aye, and by night also, so far
as most of us are concerned. If I could spell them, I
should be like Goldsmith's schoolmaster, over-burdened
with learning; if I could pronounce them, and my
readers within hearing, it might be dangerous to the
sensitive mechanism of their cultivated ears. One thing,
however, I must not forget to note before we make our
parting bow to the strong-minded ladies. The Five
Sisters, sitting in their statuesque beauty at the head of
Loch Duich, have some at least of their treasures at their
feet. Among these, none is fairer than the lower end of
Glenshiel. Just at the feet of one of the Sisters, the river,
emerging from a broad dark tarn, begins its ripple and
warble again to beguile the tedium of the way; dances
forward between pebbly shores and hanging branches;
then plunges beneath a high-backed bridge into a long

deep pool, whose rugged sides are dripping with foliage; and at length, having sung its swan-song between heathery banks, falls to sleep in the dark waters which have come to meet it from the ocean. There, too, on either hand, are wild crags and knolls, interspersed with larch and fir, where you must tread knee-deep in heather or breast-high in ferns. Loch Duich has both beauty and majesty; for if the lower reaches have a beauty which rises upward toward majesty, the lower show us majesty having her feet clothed with beauty.

Now, reader, what would you like to study or enjoy, if happily you should visit Loch Duich? Are you in love with botany? Space would fail me to tell of the roses, and irises, and hyacinths, and many other wild flowers which adorn her shores and banks. Are you a devotee of geology? You may study the gneiss and schist formations of the Highlands to your heart's content, or discuss with yourself, or perhaps better still, with some expert friend, whether Loch Duich is a depressed valley or an encroachment of the sea. Are you fond of mountaineering? You may climb Ben Attow, which I have never heard of anybody having done, provided no gamekeeper turns you back for disturbing the deer, and you have made a special defensive alliance with the Meteorological Office against mist and rain. Are you an artist? What glorious subjects and effects may here be found! You have mountain and sky, loch and river—rainbows which smile as they creep along the hill-sides, and mists which die of their very reluctance to depart. Do you delight in antiquities? Learn and, better still, write the story of the wild Eilandonan; or find out for me if it be true that the very name of Gruagach, above Totaig, denotes a yellow-haired Apollo among the Celts, and that his temple stood there on the hill-side. Is boating one of your pastimes? You may indulge it here with impunity, if you take care that your boldness be not greater than your prudence. Are you interested in social politics? Most of the solid earth you see belonged once to the Clan Mackenzie; now it is part of an enormous deer forest, rented by an American millionaire. "The clan is broken" indeed; but is "the estate improved"? Are you a student of the weather? If the wind be from the north or east, you may have tracks of lovely sunshine; if it come from the west or south-west, as it commonly does, you may patiently press your nose against the window panes for a week, with intervals for sleep, and see no more of Loch Duich than the breadth of your own street or duck-pond in the far south. Is there any one who questions the wit or humour of the Celtic race? Here I can smite him hip and thigh with irresistible proof. Let him turn to the statistical account of the parish, and there he will find a worthy clergyman mildly suggesting that "generally speaking, the climate may be termed damp." That man was a humourist, conscious or unconscious, of the first water, as I think I shall clearly show before this chapter is at an end.

Let me close this inquiry by asking, Would you like to learn the language of the people? In the light of an incident which springs into memory among many more from Loch Duich, no process or task of the kind could

well be easier. In a humble home one day a worthy native
of more than middle age undertook to give a lady visitor
a lesson in Gaelic. The text-book, as frequently in the
Highlands, and in this case very naturally, was the
Bible itself. Opening the sacred book at the beginning
of Genesis, he said,

"Now, ma'am, I'll read this to you in the Gaulic, and
you'll see yourself how will it go."

Then, with the usual solemn intonation, and an appealing, almost triumphant, glance toward the lady at
every clause, he read the first few verses of the chapter,
and paused to watch the effect. Only one word more
was needed to clinch the lesson home, and it came.

"Now, ma'am, if you'll take your own Bible, and turn
up that chapter, and read it in English, you'll see that
it's just the self and same thing."

Perhaps we should here add the mystic letters Q. E. F.,
signifying "which was to be done." To all appearance,
the worthy man believed then, and perhaps believes still,
that from that hour the lady knew at least three or four
verses of Gaelic. How could it be otherwise after so
plain and conclusive a demonstration ? Notwithstanding, having made recent inquiries, I find that the lady
was then, and alas ! still remains, quite unconscious of
her happy acquirement.

Many curious stories might be culled from the unwritten records of Loch Duich and the district around.
We shall first take one, which, from its very substance,
must be very ancient indeed—as old at least as the
glacial period, which probably began before the birth of

the most venerable native now alive in Kintail. In
Loch Alsh, a few miles from the entrance to Loch Duich,
a small black rock, called Clach Chuir, or the Putting-
Stone, lies at some distance from the shore. Strange to
say, we are told most precisely how it came there.
Somewhere near by there lived a giant—name now
unknown—who possessed a castle of some sort, and
in that castle kept a dungeon for the accommodation of
friends or foes, it mattered little which. These are no
more than conjectures; but we are distinctly informed
that the giant had a prisoner who, somehow or other,
made his escape from confinement. Apparently he was a
good swimmer, for he took to the water at once, hoping to
cross the loch in safety. The giant sallied forth in pursuit, but was unable to swim after the fugitive. Vexed
at his own impotence, and fuming with rage, he did the
worst he could. Casting his eye upon a great boulder
upon the hill-side, he used it as his putting-stone, and
hurled it at the swimmer far out upon the loch. Whether
it was a hit or a miss we are not told; but there, in the
sea, lies the boulder to this day, and wears its appropriate
name. Whether there exist any parish records of that
period, and whether, if extant, they contain the full
Christian names and other details relating to this story,
I am unable to say, because I have made no inquiry.
Perhaps the most we can say of it is this:

> " The story is told by legends old,
>   And by withered dame and sire,
> When they sit secure from the winter's cold
>   All round the evening fire."

Another story—much more modern—accords, at least
in one particular, with our experience.   More than once,
on the high ground behind Eilandonan, an ill-tempered
bull, lord of a herd of cattle, interfered in the most un-
called-for manner with our artistic studies.   We resented
his impudent conduct, because, evidently, his criticism
was not likely to be impartial, much less friendly.   Besides, few people like to have another, especially a
stranger—especially an angry bull—looking over their
shoulder when at work.   What I wish, however, frankly to
confess is this, that I never did, and never could, emulate
the courage of a certain one in this district who came face
to face with a similar difficulty, namely, a furious bull.
This hero was a Romish priest who resided in Kintail.   If I
mistake not, he had spent part of his life in Spain, where
he had apparently learnt something of the art of bull-
taming.   His method was simple enough, but could only
be executed by a man, such as he seems pre-eminently to
have been, of prodigious strength and agility.   By the
way, I remember that long ago the question was raised
in junior debating clubs, " If a man has a wild bull by
the tail, whether is it more prudent to hold on or let
go ? "   The reverend father of whom I am speaking
would have said, "Hold on," for observe how he dealt
with one very vicious and dangerous animal near Loch
Duich.   Catching the brute by the tail, which he whipped
firmly round his left hand, he wielded in his right a
stout rope on which he had twisted a series of knots.
So the fun began.   Round and round a wide field he
drove and lashed, and lashed and drove, the maddened

foaming creature. When it attempted to turn upon
him, he nimbly leapt aside from reach of its horns, and
then by way of reprisal made the chastisement more
severe than ever. In the end, bruised in body and
broken in temper, the creature stood beside him like a
lamb, and was never more a terror in the neighbourhood.
This story was told me on authority not at all inferior
to what is common in like instances; but if you doubt
it, please send me your card privately, and I shall do my
best to procure you an introduction either to the priest
or to the bull. You will then be able to ascertain for
yourself from one of the two principal parties concerned
—whichever you think likely to be most approachable—
the actual truth and precise details of the incident.

The day of our farewell to Loch Duich was most
memorable, not perhaps to the world at large, nor even
to the natives whose friendship and good will we had
secured, but certainly to ourselves. In the morning we
crossed the Dornie Ferry, and having slowly and tediously
surmounted the mountains behind Loch Alsh, came down
by a steep and dangerous descent to Strome Ferry on
Loch Carron. We had arranged that some friends from
a distance should meet us there, as it was the railway
terminus, and that we should spend the day together.
Loch Carron is a fine " voe," as it would be called in
Shetland, and both sides from the narrow strait at Strome
outward to the open sea are richly varied and picturesque. The day was bright and sunny; and we fully
enjoyed the society both of our friends and of mother
nature. After a comfortable dinner in the hotel, there

was of course an affecting parting—I refer specially to the
ladies—at the station, and then we were alone again to
wend our way back over the hills to the mouth of Loch
Duich.   For these bare statements and dry details I
must crave indulgence ; the reader, if patient, will see
their significance by and by.   We had come to Strome
by the mail cart in the morning ; we returned by the
same means of conveyance in the evening.   Between the
seats at our backs during the return journey, there lay
the innocent-looking Post Office bags with the tight-
bound cord and splutter of red wax upon their headless
necks.   Little did we dream what cause of strange experience, what seeds of anxiety and yet of mirth also,
what a summons to sleepless adventure, these dun-
coloured sacks concealed in their folds, not for others,
not for some unknown one somewhere, but for ourselves !
    When we arrived at our destination, we did ample jus-
tice to an abundant meal, and during its progress chatted
over the happy events of the day.   About eight o'clock
at night, when we had settled cosily round the fire, the
post arrived, bringing a telegram which had travelled
with us, although we could not possibly suspect it, all
the way from Strome Ferry.   It bore the unwelcome
tidings that a relative in the south had met with a serious
accident, and that we must return from the Highlands
immediately.   The wording of the message was strong,
and naturally alarmed us in no small degree.   Happily
the final issue of the mishap was perfect recovery, so that
now we can look back upon our journey from Loch Duich
with more mirth than sadness.   In less than a minute

our minds were made up to catch the train at Strome
Ferry at five o'clock next morning. A messenger was
sent off to Balmacarra for the mail cart to convey us
for the third time over the same hills ; our bill for
board and lodging was ordered, and all our goods and
chattels, down even to the unfinished manuscript of a
Highland story, stuffed without care or ceremony into
boxes and portmanteaus. By nine o'clock we were over
the Ferry, and waiting eagerly for our conveyance.
Already we had begun to taste the sweets of our
journey. Burdened clouds from the Skye mountains sailed swiftly overhead as we hurried from our
door to the pier, and during our brief passage across
poured out upon us the very fulness of their hearts.
They were determined to give us a last benefit, and to
saturate us with the remembrance of one dominant and
seldom absent feature of the scenery to which we were
bidding adieu. Shortly before ten, the mail-cart arrived,
and we were glad to find that the driver, a genuine Celt all
over—make, morals, and manners—had yoked a fresh
horse to the work. I sat in front beside her Majesty's
servant, into whose private pocket the proceeds of this
extra trip would be cheerfully welcomed ; while the others
had somehow or other managed, for the better shelter,
to get huddled in where the mail-bags had been before.
Though we could see almost nothing, the stages of the
journey were most distinctly marked—first, a mile or two
of level road among cultivated fields in one of which the
valiant priest had so skilfully tamed the bull ; then a long
monotonous ascent—steep and unbroken—to an eleva-

B

tion of a thousand feet ; then a weary, winding tract of
mountain-top and moor ; and finally, a rattling descent
upon Strome and its hotel, nearly four hours after the start.
The route it is possible to describe more or less in-
telligibly ; the weather utterly baffles my poor powers
of expression.   Of course, it is the proper thing to say
that the rain " fell in torrents " from the time we left
Dornie Ferry till we arrived at Strome, and indeed long
after.   Equally of course, I must declare that we were
" drenched to the skin."   I might even be more specific
and affirm that there was scarcely one dry square inch of
clothing upper or under, nor of skin beneath, even to the
soles of our feet, upon any one of us.   The gusty wind made
a plaything of the rain, squeezing it through the texture of
umbrellas, or scooping it cunningly in below them ; dashing it now upon one cheek, now, in the wantonness of sport,
upon the other ; filling little lochs and tarns—copies of
those we were passing—in the folds of waterproofs and
shawls ; blowing away from our noses and ears the drip
which, had it been winter, would have crystallised
into beautiful icicles—its own organ-like bass being all
the while a fitful accompaniment to the hissing, bubbling,
spluttering waters as they fell.   There were no showers—
the plural is out of place—there was but one shower, alone
and indivisible.   After careful thought and calculation,
I estimate its dimensions as follows : height, say 5000
feet, many of the mountains within its range being from
3000 to 4000 ; breadth, a diameter of 100 miles more
or less, the area covered being probably circular in form ;
length, not less than twenty-four hours—a very moderate

calculation for the district ; depth—well, there I confess myself at a loss, because it might vary greatly according to the nature of the strata underneath the surface. This last point I may illustrate by stating that in this very district the fairies once ordered a native to remove a new house he was building, because the drip from the eaves was falling right down the " lum " (Anglicè, chimney) of their underground dwelling. If that be true, who can tell how far down a long-continued rain may sink even below the level of the abodes of the " guid folk ? " Allow me to say that I have always had in my own mind a scientific difficulty about that night's rainfall, which I now express for the first time. We know that there is always a certain amount of air in water, while in any ordinary shower there must be a good deal of free air also between the drops. Now, on the night in question, I am very doubtful if there was any air at all between the drops. Where then did all the free air go to, where did it find room, all that which should in ordinary circumstances have stretched over the wide area of the shower, as described in the above estimate ? To that problem I shall be glad to receive answers from experts, or indeed from any quarter whatever.

During this memorable journey over the hills, our worthy old driver did all that he could to make us happy. He did not fail to remind us of certain horrors connected with a haunted burn which at one stage of the journey roared along by the way-side. Most carefully also did he point out the spot—just on the watershed—where a grim and ghastly gallows used to

stand, and on which many a poor wretch had swung to
and fro on the breeze.   This was a sweet suggestion, on
a midnight of darkness, storm, and rain.   I tried to im-
prove the occasion by thinking of the poor lost traveller
in some foreign land who, when he came in sight of a
gallows, exclaimed in a transport of joy, " Thank God, I'm
in a civilised country."   As to the spot pointed out by the
driver, I fear that, owing to the rain, I should not recognise it again.   But—to proceed—I must now plunge,
as we did by coming down the hill, into yet deeper and
sadder experiences.   We at length arrived at the Strome
Ferry Hotel some time after one in the morning, and were,
I am sure, both thankful and hopeful.   Happy memories
of our excellent dinner there eleven hours before led us
not only to expect, but to be confident, that we had every
comfort in prospect.   With a few brief strokes, for they
are very painful, must I pass over the next half-hour of
agony and anger.   We rung and waited, rung again and
waited, rung twenty times and waited, but, as in the
case of the prophets of Baal, there was no voice nor any
that answered.   We used every tone of menace and en-
treaty.   We threw showers of gravel at the windows—in
front, where the old driver thought the master's bedroom
was—behind, where the maids were supposed to be
sleeping.   All was in vain.   Not a sound could we hear,
not even a groan nor an oath ; even the last would
have been most welcome.   What more could we do ?   I
had already torn away the brass handle and bell-plate at
the front door, and they hung dejected on the stonework,
like a modest lily drooping its head.   All was yet in

vain ; and there were still fifty miles of rain-cloud to
come over from Skye. We were sunken in despair, but
not more deeply than the local old man himself, whose
familiar voice might, we thought, surely have been
known. What could it all mean ? Welcomed and
feasted in the afternoon sunlight ; now shut out in the
cold and wet of midnight! What had we done to
provoke this change ? Even conscience, so justly ready
to grumble at all times, could give no reply, for we had
paid every penny of our debts at Loch Duich, even to
the last postage stamp. Of course, I thought of writing
at once to the *Times ;* but that could be done next day.
At last, when we turned our hopeless heads away from
the hotel, a gleam of light fell upon our misery—the
sweet bright star of hope—in a window of the railway
station. At once we were drawn to it, luggage and all,
as with silken or golden bands, and it did not prove either
false or cold. We found a porter at the ticket office waiting for the arrival of a fish steamer from Stornoway. To
him we confided our sorrows, and he proved to be a
man of singular humanity and kindness. In fact, he
would scarcely accept any acknowledgment of his
services afterwards. He opened the waiting-room, lit
the gas, and—what was still better—a roaring fire ; gave
us in our luggage ; drew down the blinds ; and with much
sympathy told us to make ourselves comfortable till
dawn of day. We had no food with us except a small
jar of prunes, and of these one of the party demolished
the lion's share. But we had something better than
food—a warm fire, and the opportunity of changing our
clothing. We had little or no sleep ; but when the

morning broke over the hills, and turned the sombre blind of the waiting-room into a blazing orange, we were not sorry, after paying our bill, to gather up our possessions and leave Loch Carron by the morning train at five. One of our poets—I spare him the mention of his name—moralizes to the effect that, in our journey through life, we often find " the warmest welcome in an inn." What an egregious mistake! I speak from personal experience when I say that, in the very respect he mentions, an inn is not to be compared with the waiting-room of a railway station !

One word more must be added. We have long ago freely and fully forgiven the people of the hotel. We have done so, because ethically that is the right and proper thing to do, but also because they really had a good excuse. In connection with the fish traffic, bodies of men, porters and others, frequently arrived at Strome at or after midnight, and came to the hotel demanding refreshments, and sometimes creating disturbance. To stop this nuisance, it was resolved to open the doors to no one during the night under any pretext or inducement whatever—a decision as prudent as it was natural. Looking at it philosophically, our experience was only an illustration and proof of the solidarity of the human race, many of whom have to suffer for the faults and errors of others. In that great underlying fact, all tribes and nations, all creeds and colours, have an equal share,

" For mankind are one in spirit and an instinct bears along
  Round the earth's electric circle, the swift flash of right or wrong ;
  Whether conscious or unconscious, yet humanity's vast frame
  Through its ocean-sundered fibres, feels the gush of joy or shame ;
  In the gain or loss of one race, all the rest have equal claim."

From Photo. by G. W. Wilson.

ENTRANCE TO BLACK ROCK, NOVAR, ROSS-SHIRE.

CHAPTER II.

THE BLACK ROCK, ROSS-SHIRE.

On the eastern side of the County of Ross, and skirting the shores of the Cromarty Firth, lie the parishes of Kiltearn and Alness, both richly pastoral on their lower levels, both wildly mountainous in the inland regions above and behind. The length of their united coast line is not more than nine or ten miles, but their western boundaries, widening as they recede from the Firth, are lost far out of sight in the central solitudes of the county. The dividing line between these neighbour parishes is the river Aultgraat, which in Gaelic means the ugly or fearsome burn. That picturesque stream takes its rise in the dark waters of Loch Glass, which itself lies almost hidden beneath the northern shadows of the massive Ben Wyvis. Its early course, between the lower moorland slopes of that monarch mountain and the precipitous rocky sides of Ben Diollaide,—the Saddle mountain,—is tame and peaceful—here a rippling, gurgling current over a stony beach—there a drowsy crawl through a long, dark pool, edged by banks of heather and bog myrtle. By and by, a few miles from the loch, its career becomes more stirring and eventful. Approaching the outer edge of a wooded knoll, it suddenly stumbles in among rugged

cliffs and giant boulders, which force the angry and reluctant torrent to bend aside abruptly to the left. Then,
after a series of wild cascades, the last wildest and
grandest of all, it sinks, panting and fuming, into the
bottom of a deep ravine, one side clothed with lofty larch
trees, the other with rugged, stony banks of heather.
These are the picturesque, but little known, Falls of the
Aultgraat, of which, in due course, we must speak in
more detail. For several miles more, ever growing in
volume, the river runs on, by the yellow cliffs and scars,
through the meadows and fields, of the open Glen Glass.
Then comes the singular and most impressive feature of
its scenery—the great crisis in their history through
which all its waters must pass—the chasm of the Black
Rock. Let me here turn aside for a sentence or two to
say that the name Black Rock is a most unsuitable one.
Those who have never seen it will at once picture to
themselves one solitary mass of rock, with some peculiar
interest attached to it, instead of a long, deep, narrow
ravine, as is the reality. Gorge, chasm, ravine,—any one
of these is more truly descriptive of the awe-inspiring
phenomenon, though none expresses at all adequately its
quite unique features.

Glen Glass does not, like most others of the name,
open outward to the sea. Three miles at least from the
Cromarty Firth, the wide-spreading sides of the glen
curve rapidly inward until the steep banks on either side
press nearer and still nearer to the channel of the river.
At length the unsuspecting waters come face to face with
two lofty rocky portals, between which they must plunge

whether they will or no ; and then—farewell for a mile and a half to sunshine and calm and liberty ! The grim gateway, which never tells its secret to the waters as they come dancing along, closes in upon them at once, and forms the entrance to a chasm long and deep, between whose narrow and sunless walls the stream must fight its troubled way to the open sky and the song of birds and the bright flowers, which, as yet, are far away. At the further end, the lofty iron gates, much like those facing the glen above, unfold themselves amid a mass of foliage, and bid good speed to the waters as they start again on their race to the sea. The chasm from end to end lies in a deep depression, having a steep pine-covered wood on the one hand, and the sloping fields of a fine farm on the other. Both edges of the gorge, which here and there almost kiss each other at the surface, are clothed with trees and shrubs, and decked with brown heather and wild flowers ; and no stranger would suspect even its presence until he stood upon the very brink, but for the hoarse, sullen roar of the imprisoned waters, deep down almost under his feet. The depth of the chasm varies at different points, but cannot be less, during greater part of its course, than one hundred and ten to one hundred and thirty feet, while the sides in many places are no more than seventeen feet apart. The simplest means of sounding the ravine is by the clear drop of a stone from the edge above to the water below ; but there are very few places indeed, where a straight and unbroken fall can be secured.

Approaching the brink from the pathway, and throwing

one's arm round a sturdy branch, what do we see? Peering downward into the darkness, far, far beneath our feet, between the gruesome walls, we catch glimpses, in spots or streaks of flickering light, of the rushing, whirling, boiling torrent below. Though I venture to claim that I know more of the chasm than most people, no words that come to me can describe the infinite freaks and strange fortunes of the waters, "cribbed, cabined, and confined" in this pit-like channel. Sometimes they rush forward straight and strong between two opposing ledges; sometimes they stumble, suddenly and at unawares, over an obstructing ridge ; anon they whirl in serpent-like coils round and round a foaming caldron ; yet again they plunge into a pit or tunnel in the rock to emerge again —no one knows where, and no one knows how. Very sad too and weary—ever sad and weary—are the burdens of song they bear. Heard from a distance, the voices of the chasm are but one low dull murmur, but, if you listen attentively, sympathetically, as you go along the pathway, you may catch at intervals every note in the whole gamut of sad passion and wild emotion. Now we hear a sulky roar, as of a wild beast crawling from his den ; again, a weary sigh, as of a hapless hopeless lover ; at times it seems an eerie wail as of an infant alone in the night ; at times a wild dirge, sinking and swelling, as when the clan bewails its fallen chief. But while you look for glimpses of the waters, and hearken to their ever-changing music, do not forget to mark how wild and grand are the rocky walls of this deep dark rent in mother earth. They present every possible variety of form and combination to be found in the Old Red Conglomerate. Here, there is a sloping ledge as smooth as pudding-stone can ever be ; there, a bluff corner behind which the shadows are black as night. More frequently to be found than perhaps any other form is a scooped-out hollow like the valve of a gigantic shell, sometimes widening into bays, sometimes deepening into dripping caves. Mingling with these in such confusion and strange succession as cannot be told, are innumerable capes and corries, gulfs and groins, columns and buttresses, fissures and crevices—their variety and mystery adding fresh charm to each new reach of the channel that is visible to mortal eye. Clothing both sides of the chasm all along its course are shrubs, and grasses, and wild flowers of many a genus and hue, while many varieties of the matchless fern cling to the overhanging cliffs, and mock the almost irresistible longing to pluck them and carry off as treasure trove their exquisite and delicate fronds.

Such are a few, feebly pictured, of the striking features of the chasm. But there come times—ever and anon, at wide intervals—when all these, well marked though they be, seem blotted, one might think irretrievably, out of existence. It is when winter snows, or autumn rains, have streamed down in glittering silver from the mountains round Glen Glass and have raised the Aultgraat into high flood. Then the surging waters, panting passionately for the ocean, rise half-way or sometimes more up the walls of the chasm, covering all its blackness out of sight, smothering all its varied voices in one

continuous thunderous roar ; and then they sweep down
in the resistless rush of their tawny flood every loose
boulder and tree stump which lies, and may long have
lain, hidden in its many and mysterious recesses.
Whither, you may ask, are these waifs and strays
borne ? Whither, as to their final destination, no man
can tell ; but in the first instance, they are swept out of
the chasm and down to the centre of the open arena—
the basement of that most lovely amphitheatre—where
the Aultgraat emerges from its imprisonment. What
a scene of picturesque beauty is that ! The waters,
wearied-looking after their long struggle in the cruel
darkness, creep out, almost motionless, between two
pillars of rock, whose capitals are real foliage, and
whose feet are fringed with foam. Then they settle
down to rest them in a broad brown pool, whose
inner end is hidden from view among the jutting
corners of rock, while its outer margin sweeps round
in a graceful curve at our feet. What a change—
so bright and happy—in the fortunes of the stream !
A sweet, almost sacred, repose settles on its face as it
breathes again the free air of heaven.. Pleased and
patient, it suffers the strings of green leaves above to
mirror themselves on its bosom. It delights to lap with
a gentle kiss the feet of the brown rocks, which have
stood off from one another to permit of its release. Let
us now look round about and up above us. On every
hand we are shut in by high, steep, and richly-wooded
banks, which open widely and cheerfully to the sky.
Near the chasm they have deep, shady recesses and

clefts, the loved home and shelter of many varieties of
fern and other wild flowers. The conglomerate pillars
which overlook the pool are crowned with waving foliage,
and the airy sprays stretch across and almost meet over
the languid waters. Looking backward from the edge
of the pool where we now stand, we cannot see, though
we may guess, at what point the stream, starting on its
career again, makes its escape among the trees. From
out the chasm in seasons of high flood are tossed great
boulders and shapeless masses of stone, which are piled
up in rugged confusion beyond the margin of the great
pool. A few small trees and shrubs and wild flowers
lead a precarious life among the mammoth blocks, which
seem the debris of some primeval quarry, or the unused
material of some ancient temple. Over and among these
masses we are permitted to-day—for we dare not be
here in flood time—to wander as we will, and watch the
waters play in their changing moods and manners, and
guess as best we can whence these great stones came.
Perhaps some of them were first torn from their parent
strata away among the heights of Torridon and Gruinard
on the Atlantic seaboard. Ploughed up it may be by
glacial currents, or worn down from mountain sides,
the larger blocks may have come hither a far journey;
while the smaller stones, washed away from field or
heathery banks, lie now among roots and branches which
almost seem as if they would dare to grow again. There
they all lie, in one bleached, broken mass, and shall lie
till the next great flood lifts and scatters them again.

Perhaps, while we sit here among the boulders, you

may ask how the chasm of the Black Rock came to be
formed? There are two chief theories, differing widely
in many respects, each of which can boast of at least one
great name in its support. Being no geologist, my wisdom is to state both views as briefly and simply as I can,
and let the reader choose which he considers most in accordance with evidence and common sense. Hugh Miller,
the noble stone-mason of Cromarty in his early days,
speaks of the chasm as a gigantic fault or fissure in the
Conglomerate—first filled with boulder clay or some
form of rocky debris, and afterwards, slowly but steadily,
washed down and washed out by the raging river. Professor Geikie thinks the channel has been water-worn
from first to last, from top to bottom, even out of the
stern Conglomerate itself. Apparently the extreme hard-
ness of the rock in the former case, and the scooped form
of the walls in the latter, supply the main arguments on
the respective sides. Under either theory, what a vete-
ran world is this in which we live! How many ages have
gone by since the unwearied Aultgraat began its strange
task? It is doubtful if the attrition of the rocks has
amounted all over to even one inch in several centuries.
Who then can venture to prophesy backwards to the
origin of the work? Having travelled in thought to the
ages now far behind us, we may surely, without harming
anyone, indulge in a little innocent speculation. Perhaps, in the far back days of the Olympian Court, old
Mother Ge—the Earth—gave some offence to one of the
assembled gods. Burning to avenge himself, the angry
notable struck her a terrific blow with his battle axe,

and the long, deep, lacerated wound remains to this day
in the fearsome chasm of the Aultgraat. The trees and
shrubs have done their best to hide their Mother's sorrow;
but the prying eyes of nineteenth-century travellers will
not be cheated of their delights for nothing.

Before dealing with incidents or stories connected with
the Black Rock itself, here is one from each of the two
parishes which meet between its banks.

Among the Highland clans long ago, there were frequent and sore disputes—often ending in bloodshed—as
to questions of territories and boundaries. Not a few of
these arose in spite of many efforts and varied methods,
by which the interested parties sought to prevent their
recurrence. One device which was sometimes practised
—whether in Ross-shire or not, I am not certain—was as
peculiar as it was cruel. The chiefs and leaders of two
clans, many of them old men, met upon the marches of
their respective lands. Each band took with them a
number of growing lads from their families. When the
companies arrived at the spot from which they were to
draw the frontier line, they stripped bare the backs of
the young men, and then, forming a procession of which
these were the central line, lashed and scourged their
stripling sons along every foot of the track as they went.
Crawling along, pained and bleeding, under this process
of torture, it was thought certain that every step of
the march line must be cut deeply, indelibly, on the
memories of the rising generation. When they, in their
turn, came to be chiefs and leaders of the clans, they
would still remember their bitter lesson, and the way in

which it was taught them. Methinks I hear some
kindly reader exclaim, "What a barbarous, hideous
practice! What cruel wretches these chiefs and clansmen must have been!" Not so fast, my good friend!
Some of us, who do not yet care to be called old, know
something on a small scale of the same system. What
about those venerable appliances of education, the
tawse and the cane? Are there none of them seen in
schools now-a-days? Are they all in the Antiquarian
Museums? I fear they are not; but my business now
is with the past. Some of us know that by means of
these sweet instruments of torture, an attempt at least
was made—whether successful or not—to carve into us
the difference between vulgar and proper fractions, and
between a subject with its attributes and a predicate
with its extensions. My own feeling is, that the system
did not work very well; but of course I am only one
among very many. At all events, it did not perfectly
serve its purpose in the North, for in spite of it, quarrels
often arose and grew serious. On one occasion a great
dispute fell out between the Baron of Fowlis, the chief of
the Munroes, on the one hand, and the Laird of Tulloch
on the other—the question at issue being one of boundary. Let me digress for a moment to mention a curious
circumstance about the Munroes of Fowlis. It is said
that they first obtained a charter or deed securing them
their lands on condition that at any time of the year
they should on demand present the king with a snow-
ball from Ben Wyvis. They are never likely to lose their
possessions through any failure as to the condition, for I

know that snow ball fights have taken place on Ben Wyvis
on the very last days of July. But to return. The
crucial point between Fowlis and Tulloch was whether a
certain stone lay on the lands of the one or of the other.
On an appointed day arbiters were chosen and witnesses
called. The case proceeded in the rough and ready
fashion common to such tribunals. At length, one of
the men of Tulloch came forward, and boldly planting
his feet close by the stone in dispute, exclaimed, "The
soil on which I stand belongs to Tulloch." For some
reason or other, the Munroes doubted his testimony and
suspected stratagem of some sort, so they threw him on
the ground and stripped off his shoes. These articles
were discovered to be thickly lined with earth within.
Further inquiry and perhaps a little gentle torture
elicited the confession that the earth had been taken that
morning from Tulloch garden, so that he might be able
to swear as he had done, and yet escape, as he hoped,
the guilt of perjury. His punishment was as speedy as
it was sharp. They dragged him to the fatal stone itself,
and there—whether beside it or on it, we are not told—
chipped off first one and then the other of his ears. He
was spared the infliction of hearing the curses which
followed him into disgrace. The "Stone of the Ears"
still remains in the uplands of Kiltearn.

The parish of Alness is most extensive; and even in
its remoter regions there are glens which contain a fair
sprinkling of crofter families. Nominally, the whole
population is under the care of the parish minister; but
most people know well that, at the time of the famous

c

Disruption of 1843, the great mass of the people left the
Establishment, and cast in their lot with the Free Church.
The clergy who remained in the State Church were called
" Moderates," because, in the opinion of the people, they
were chargeable with lukewarmness both as to Christian
doctrine and Church principles.   One of these was presented to the parish of Alness not long after the Disruption, and though his own congregation did not probably
exceed a dozen, resolved to act upon the principle that he
was everybody's minister whether they would or no.
Following out this idea, he began a systematic visitation,
and called upon all and sundry, even upon those who
might be called adversaries.   It happened that one day
he visited a Free Church elder, who was no friend of the
" Moderates."   The minister did his very best to be
affable and conciliatory, but his reception was cold, and,
in fact, little more than civil.   At length, without any
special intention in the act, he drew his snuff-box from
his pocket, and invited the elder to make trial of its
contents.   A decided thaw set in immediately.

" Oh, ye tak' snuff, do ye ? " said the Free Kirk man,
yielding to a gentle smile.

" Oh, yes," replied his visitor, somewhat afraid lest the
admission might lead him into trouble.   " I take snuff;
but what of that ? "

" Weel," said the elder, with a look of satisfaction to
which probably the excellent snuff contributed its full
share, " that's the first sign o' grace I've seen aboot ye."

" Sign of grace ! " rejoined the minister, with no little
surprise, but glad that a promising vein of conversation

had at length been opened. "How do you make out that the habit of taking snuff is a sign of grace?"

"Nothing easier," said the elder, with a knowing twinkle in his eye. "Don't you remember that in the temple of old all the snuffers were of pure gold, which denotes the best of all qualities?"

Was ever proof so cogent or conclusive? And yet, somehow, it fairly upset the gravity of the minister. Perhaps it was the breezy freshness of the logic which shook his sides with laughter. What a pity there is no record of the sequel of the interview!

But we must return to the Black Rock itself.

No one will wonder that legend and story have gathered thickly around scenes so impressive and mysterious. Never can I think of the Black Rock without waking into memory the image of the Lady of Balcony. Her tragic adventure and fate have been admirably told by Hugh Miller in his "Scenes and Legends of the North of Scotland." By all means read the story there, if you can lay your hands upon the volume. For the benefit of those who have not within reach Miller's full and graphic narrative, let me tell the story as briefly as I can. The Lady of Balcony, a property down by the shores of the Cromarty Firth, spent much of her time wandering to and fro on the banks of the Aultgraat. The fear-haunted neighbourhood of the dark chasm possessed for her a peculiar fascination. Her companion in these rambles was a simple Highland girl, who was deeply attached to her mistress. One night, just as the sun was setting, the lady terrified her maid by proposing to enter the chasm not far above the great pool. In spite of all the girl's entreaties and efforts to detain her, the mistress was determined to have her way, and shaking free of her maid, stepped downward through the brush-wood by the dizzy brink of the gorge. Just then a tall stranger, dressed in green, came from behind, and, speaking in commanding tones, pressed his services upon the Lady, and led her down into the rocky shadows. A few moments before she disappeared, she flung her household keys upward to her maid. They struck a gigantic granite boulder—a traveller ages ago from the far west—and left upon its surface their deep and permanent impress. The poor girl, distracted with alarm and grief, returned to tell her sad story ; she saw her loved mistress no more.

One day, many years after, an angler named Donald, servant to a lady who lived near by, had been unusually successful in filling his basket with trout. Selecting so many to carry to his mistress, he hid a goodly number under a bush, intending to present them to his mother. On his return he found that the trout which he had left at the Black Rock were gone, but he could trace their scales among the weeds along the very brink. Being brave, and at the same time angry and curious, he carefully followed the track, and after many a dangerous slip and dark turn found himself down close by the raging current. There, in a gloomy cavern, its entrance guarded by two dogs, he found the Lady of Balcony busily en-gaged in the homely duty of baking. Donald entered her strange abode, and after some conversation strongly urged her to make her escape; but such was the dread inspired by her mysterious gaoler, that she would not listen to any suggestion in the direction of such an attempt. At length Donald bade the Lady farewell, and prepared to leave the cavern. Springing back between the two dogs when the Lady flung a lump of leaven to each of them, he returned to the upper world again to tell of his strange adventure. Never since that hour has the Lady of Balcony been seen; but the natives often speak of her and her sad fate. Their story—perhaps their belief—is, that her cruel gaoler is none other than "Black Donald" himself, the Prince of Darkness; and when they see the white mist rising over the tree-tops above the chasm, they whisper, as they toil in the neighbouring fields, that the Lady is busy at her old occupation in her cavern home.

Once upon a time—how long ago, I shall not say,—I formed one of a happy party—chiefly young people of both sexes—who visited the Black Rock. After spending some time by the black pool where the chasm terminates, we took the pathway which runs by its side all the way upward to the glen. Skirting the northern bank, the first object worthy of notice was the great boulder on which the keys of Balcony so decisively made their mark. We felt that it would be interesting to see and examine with one's own eyes evidence—tangible, sensible, evidence, which might confirm the truth of the legend. If such evidence were abundant and valuable, we should have the means of convincing any persons who might be disposed to smile and shake their sceptical heads at the story. Alas, that so many now-a-days do

not scruple to question what is venerable and sacred!
To us thus pondering, two difficulties presented themselves.   In the first place, we were on the wrong side of
the chasm—or rather the boulder very stupidly was so,
that is, for us ; and none of us felt inclined to emulate
the adventurous spirits who had climbed across upon trees
where the branches met and mingled over the gloomy
abyss.   You may also if you like take it for granted that
we did not make the attempt because we should have to
leave the ladies behind, which would be neither pleasant
nor polite.   Such was our first difficulty.   The other was
of a kind which would have met us even if we had succeeded in crossing the chasm.   At some time or other of
which we have no record, some one, evidently very much
stronger than any of us, had very thoughtlessly and
indeed wickedly turned the boulder upside down.   The
consequence of course is that the deep moulds in which
the keys imbedded themselves are now on the under
side, and, alas ! cannot be seen.   This is very provoking,
because it would be somewhat troublesome to reverse the
boulder again.   I am doubtful whether all our party
could have done it without some effort.   It has since
occurred to me that the evil deed may have been done
by "Black Donald" himself.   Just suppose he were
arrested by the local constable and taken to Dingwall,
there to be tried for his theft of the Lady and her deten-
tion in so miserable a captivity.   Think then of the
story as the poor maid, with many sobs, might narrate
it ; and you will at once see the grounds of my suspicion.
Trembling—perhaps for years—at the very thought of

standing at the bar of the Sheriff Court, who could have so strong a motive as he for the concealment of marks which in skilful hands might lead to a verdict of "Guilty" against him? My conjecture, therefore, is that, with such a possibility before him, he some day or other put his shoulder to the boulder, tilted it over, and left it on the bed where it now rests. If any demur to this view, I have only to remind them how valuable a little speculation and hypothesis have often been in the advancement of science.

A little further along the path we came to the spot whence of all others the most awe-inspiring glimpses of the chasm are to be obtained. Here the unearthly-looking fissure is narrower, deeper, and darker than anywhere else in its course. You may see, almost on your own level, the overhanging ledges under which rich beds of exquisite ferns find the shelter and moisture they need; then rugged corners and caves of rock, which deeper and still deeper down are involved, and their shadows with them, in almost midnight darkness; and yet again, far off and down in the very bottom of the abyss one little gleam of trembling light—the only token that the river still lives and breathes below. Just over this spot, we came to the remains of a bridge which had once spanned the darkness, and by which the natives of the glen above passed to and from the nearest village. It is said that the last to cross that bridge was a foolhardy old woman, who was on her homeward way late at night. Her only company was the peat cart in which she sat, and the Highland sheltie which wearily dragged it along. So

soon as her pony's feet were on the bridge, she began to
hear the timbers crackle and creak under her, and she
lashed her steed to greater speed. She was only saved as
by a single inch. Ere she fully reached the further end,
the whole structure had crumbled into broken wreckage
behind her, and the timbers crashed behind the wheels
of her cart like splintering ice in a treacherous thaw.
Surely hers was a case not less terrible, and even more
true, than that of the immortal Tam o' Shanter himself,
when good old Meg and he just won the key-stane of
the Brig o' Doon.

Less than twenty yards further we halted to engage in
a juvenile sport which has many attractions, even for
elderly visitors—that of hurling stones, the larger the
better, into the chasm. Almost from the moment they
leave the hand, they drop out of sight beneath the ledges
in front of you ; but you can hear them strike once,
twice, thrice, sometimes four or five times, on each side
alternately, and then sink with a sepulchral gulp into the
torrent below. Once a strong Galloway dyke ran along
for a good mile between the pathway and the fields. Now
it is all gone—pitched piecemeal, and by thousands of
hands, into the all-devouring jaws of the gorge. After
scores of smaller stones had been thrown in, we looked
all about us for larger material. At last we lit upon a
broad, flat stone lying on the bank above the path, and
two of us set about the work of dislodging it from its
bed. A large group of expectant spectators awaited the
result of our labours. In due time, as you shall presently
see, the whole company, in greater or lesser degree, reaped

the fruits of our toil. My comrade and I raised the stone between us, and—in a moment—dropped it like the proverbial hot potato. We were in horror and dismay. Right beneath the stone had been a powerful and populous nest of wasps, who now sallied forth and took the field in gallant style against the foe. A few critical moments, as in all great battles, ensued. The wasps were evidently under skilful leadership. A certain number— say, half-a-dozen, more or fewer—were told off to attack each lady and gentleman of the company, and they played their part well. Though they were my enemies on that occasion, I can now, after the heat and bitterness of the struggle are over, bear them witness that they did their duty bravely and zealously to the end. You will allow me to mention, with all modesty, that my comrade and I had the honour of being selected for special attention, and that by larger numbers than any of our friends. There may have been a reason for this—it may even have been because of some blue blood in our veins. But the engagement was over in less time than I have taken to describe it. Mankind, both male and female, fought wildly from the first, smiting their own noses and cheeks as frequently and impartially as those of the enemy. Then an unfortunate panic set in, and what might have been only a mild defeat became a rout. Never was there a more real and vivid illustration of the delicate Scotch proverb that a certain gentleman should take the hindmost. In a few brief moments, the whole army of the aggressors—for such we certainly had been—pursued by the now victorious garrison, fled in disorder and deshabille from the scene of conflict, leaving a scattered variety of hats, coats, shawls, handkerchiefs, and parasols dead upon the field. Even when one or two of us returned to gather up these lost remains, we were again assailed by skirmishers from the enemy's host. We cannot pass from the historical record of such an engagement as this without a word or two as to the cause or causes of defeat. These were, in my opinion, two : first, the superior organization of the enemy ; and, second, the fact that they were armed with weapons of precision. We had nothing but fingers, sticks, umbrellas, and articles of clothing ; they were provided with instruments of war of which you may see full descriptions in books of natural history. These things made all the difference ; and it is neither just nor fair for any man to throw out hints as to want of courage and the like in the face of the explanation which I have just given.

The Black Rock would not be ideally complete without the addition of a ghost story to its records. Such an attraction, though of a very harmless kind, I am happily able to supply, and at the same time to give the assurance that it will cost no one even an hour's sleep. Permit me first of all to say that what follows is absolute fact, relating to actual persons then living ; and if the heroine, for such she was in my young eyes, should chance to see these pages, she is greatly changed for the worse if she will not, with a merry, ringing laugh, and a twinkle in her eye, forgive the writer for the liberty he takes in recording her doings.

On the hillside, above the Black Rock, stands a

small castellated mansion-house, and near by it a farm-house with its steading and other out-buildings. At the back of the farm premises lies a small mill pond, with a row of ploughmen's cottages upon one side and their cabbage gardens upon the other. In the big house, more than thirty years ago, lived a middle-aged medical man, who had retired from the army in shattered health. His companion in this Highland retreat was an only daughter, still in the brightness of her teens, whom we shall call Miss Maxwell. She it was who acted the chief part in the scenes I have now to describe. She was moved to design and execute her pranks by impulses which can easily be understood. A daughter of the regiment, accustomed to the gay life of London West, and naturally brimful of life and fun, the mono-tonous quiet of her new home, within hearing of the weary sobbing and sighing of the Aultgraat, was more than she could endure. Her pent-up energy and bound-ing spirits must have vent in some form or other. Even riding and fishing were not sufficient, though good enough in their way. At length she found a measure of relief in some lively adventures, in which she sus-tained the double rôle of author and actor. Late one evening, as darkness was falling on the Black Rock woods and the Firth beyond, one or two of the plough-men stood by their cottage doors ready to wish each other good night, and retire to rest. Suddenly, in the gardens on the opposite side of the pond, a strange apparition presented itself, and attracted their won-dering gaze. It was a tall, white, stately figure, above middle height, with no head which could be distinguished from the body, yet crowned with four short, thick horns of the same pure snow colour as the drapery below.   To and fro among the plots of carrots and cabbages, and sometimes on the grassy bank beside the sluice, walked the unearthly-looking visitor with silent and dignified step.   The strange being seemed wholly wrapped up in thought and reverie of his or her own. Very soon all the waking inmates of the cottages were at their doors and at their wits' end besides.   No one dared to cry, Who are you? or, Where do you come from? nor did anyone attempt to approach or disturb the stately stranger.   By and by, as midnight drew near, the fairy-like figure slipped away in the deepening darkness, and was no more seen.   What sleep there was that night in the ploughmen's cottages, I cannot tell ; but the vision over the mill pond was all the talk of the fields next day.   On two points there was entire unanimity of opinion—the absolute objective reality of the figure, and the " uncanny," if not unearthly, nature of the visitation ; but beyond these all was uncertainty and conjecture.   If I remember aright, no solution of the mystery was found until, a week or two after, another startling occurrence took place.

Once more " the shades of night were falling fast," or had already fallen, for the " witching hour " of midnight was not far off, when the farmer was aroused from sleep and told that the grieve, or farm steward, wished to see him.   Not a little wondering what this might mean, the master hurried to the door.

"Well, John, what's the matter now?" was naturally the first question.

"Please, sir, 'am sorry to trouble ye, but 'am wantin' ye to come oot to the west field," said the grieve timidly, for he did not wish to make his fearful disclosure too abruptly. The master, however, was impatient.

"What for? Can't you tell, man? Out with it, and be done with it."

"Well, sir, it's my own belief that the devil is on Mettle, an' ye maun jist come an' see for yersel."

So the murder was out! Mettle was a strong, useful gray mare, which had been left, along with the other horses, in a grass field over night. Evidently there was something in the wind, and inquiry must be made; so the farmer prepared to accompany his servant, the former being not a little tickled and curious, the latter filled with misgiving and somewhat hurt that his master showed such coolness, not to say levity, of manner. Just as they were about to start from the farm-house, John appeared to hang back, as if reluctant to go. It appears he had a suggestion to make, for when the farmer asked him to come along, he modestly gave the advice,

"Please, sir, ye'd better take the gun wi' ye."

With a scornful laugh the master refused to do anything of the kind, and they made off in all haste for the scene of mystery. Certainly, the farmer did not expect to see what he did. There, in very deed and truth, was his good mare Mettle, sometimes walking quickly, sometimes trotting slowly, round the field, and on her back a long graceful figure dressed in purest white. Apparently the farmer, like a certain great writer, did not believe in ghosts because he had seen so many of them. With irreverent daring, he approached the fair vision ; and, alas ! the mystery was all too soon dispelled.

"How do you do, Mr B—— ? What a jolly night it is ! I hope you were not *very* much frightened. Say you're not angry with me, do ; there's a good man."

Need I say that it was the voice of Miss Maxwell, who jumped down from her unpaid-for seat, and heartily shook hands with the farmer. There was more of the ring of laughter than the rasping tones of anger as they left the field together. I believe the sprightly girl was forgiven on the spot, though I should not wonder if one or two words of serious counsel were edged in. This much is certain, there was not a particle of hypocrisy among the ploughmen that night. They felt very foolish, and being honest men, they looked exactly as they felt. Perhaps one of them dreamt about ghosts and guns. Next day everyone knew that Miss Maxwell was the performer in the first scene as well. The strange form she had then assumed was easily explained. Draping herself in white, she had taken a chair and turned it upside down upon her head. Over the four feet, as they stuck up in the air, she flung another sheet. Then to produce the horns, she threw up a stone, and let it fall right in between the legs of the chair. Thus did the mystery of those formidable objects come into being. The bold pranks of a lovely, but very lively, young lady are among those things which are not always "dreamt of in our philosophy."

In the early part of this chapter mention was made of the Falls of the Aultgraat, some four miles above the Black Rock ; but they deserve much fuller notice. They are, so far as I can judge, the most picturesque falls in the northern counties, with the possible exception of Glomak in Kintail, which, I am almost ashamed to say, I have not yet seen. There are two reasons why they are as yet comparatively unknown, and have, therefore, hitherto received but scanty public appreciation. In the first place, they are situated in that same glen out of which the Aultgraat passes into the dingy defile of the Black Rock, and they, of course, suffer from this proximity to a great sight. A visit to the famous chasm is enough for most people in one day, and they will scarcely thank you for telling them that there is another object of attraction four miles further up the river. Moreover, the road up the glen is on the north side, from which the falls cannot be seen to any advantage ; while the track up the south side means serious work. It involves some rough climbing, and the difficult, if not dangerous, crossing of a mountain torrent, over which there is no bridge whatever. This candid mention of the somewhat arduous nature of the journey may deter some who are not fit for it, which is good ; it will, I hope, stimulate many more to make the attempt, which will be still better. All that is wanted is a fair measure of activity and courage, which will meet with ample reward. Never yet have I heard from any who have really seen them, a different opinion of the falls from that which I have expressed above.

Having frequently acted as guide, I can, from some experience, describe the route by the south side of the river. The road, which you may join a little way above the upper end of the Black Rock, soon descends into the bottom of the glen. Take care that you quit the highway opposite a deserted house among trees by the riverside. Thence you skirt the banks of the stream among straggling bushes and shrubs, having on the right a level field, and behind it a steep, gravelly cliff, along the face of which the road wends its upward way to a plateau above. By and by, you arrive at a very remarkable suspension bridge, by which you must cross the river. Two rude pillars of stone stand on opposite sides of the noisy, bustling stream. These are crowned by rough woodwork, over which are stretched in long graceful bend threads of wire such as are used for ordinary fencing. From these again are suspended a few narrow planks of wood, which form the footway ; and so the wonderful structure is complete. Even the wind may sway it to and fro at pleasure. Might I here make a suggestion to the "authorities"—I need not name them—one which might tend to the saving of precious human life. It is this, that a weighing machine with the usual slot apparatus be erected at the near end of the bridge, because there are certain parties not of the spare order who, for their own sakes, should not be permitted to cross at all, especially if they be suspected of any suicidal tendencies; while only a limited number, say, one and a half, even of those who are of lighter capacity, should be allowed to venture at a time. Those who are fond of swing motion, lateral or perpendicular, may indulge their fancy to their hearts' content, and at their own risk, just over the middle of the stream.

When last I crossed this remarkable bridge, there were two of our party, young gentlemen, left behind, but plain directions had been given them how to follow. However, to make assurance doubly sure, we scratched a few words of further guidance on a piece of paper—the characters being Greek—and stuck them on the wire at one end of the bridge, where they could hardly fail to attract the notice of our friends. Later on, these young gentlemen did overtake us, but protested that they had never seen anything of the message. There are only two rational explanations of this circumstance. The one affects not perhaps the character, but at all events the culture, of the individuals in question. They were students at the "Toun's College" of Edinburgh. What if, notwithstanding their university training, they could not decipher the Greek letters—I have seen as much where you would not expect it—and therefore destroyed the paper to prevent the discovery of their ignorance and incapacity? Please do not tell either the retired B— or the busy B— of the Greek chair in Edinburgh! It would be a pity to burden them with so sorrowful a supposition. The second hypothesis relates to the inhabitants of the glen, and is of a more favourable and cheering nature. The question is, what became of the paper? Perhaps some native, say, a herd boy, thirsting after the heights of human knowledge, had discovered the precious fragment, and carried it off in triumph. Had it been vulgar, every-day English, he would never have fingered the worthless thing ; but the temptation of Greek—was it not the language of Sophocles and Demosthenes ?—may have been too much for his virtue. Who can for a moment doubt, if this be true, that the future prospects of classical scholarship in the Highlands—at all events in Glen Glass—are very bright indeed ?

From the rustic suspension bridge, the path struggles onward by the river side among trees and shrubs and heathery grass—its margin sprinkled with many-coloured flowers, between ferny banks and burrows both above and below. Then the track, now becoming uncertain, slants upward over broken banks to the well-defined site of an old farm, which I can well remember as the happy home of a decent and industrious crofter family. Only the sheep now wander among the fallen stones ; perhaps the deer visit them in the stress of winter. It is a case of " old homes and new tenants." Well did a speaker some years ago say, " When Christ asked, How much more then is a man better than a sheep ? he sowed the seed of a whole harvest of revolutions." Soon after passing the deserted croft, we reached the edge of a wild, deep ravine, through which roared and tumbled a sprightly mountain torrent, ever gabbling over the story of its descent from Ben Wyvis. Here all must encounter *the* difficulty of the journey. If there has been much recent rain, you had better be content with the Black Rock, for this stream will be quite impassable ; but if the weather has been fairly dry for a time, you may run your chance of getting over. As to the method, there is nothing for it but to spring from stone to stone over the rushing currents between them, and reach at length the opposite bank. If you dip one foot, or even both, in the water, and that be all your mishap, you are fortunate ; worse cases have occurred.

Mounting the steep slope now in front, you reach a grassy path along the hill side, and can hear the roar of the falls a little way in advance, and see the wooded knoll under which they hide from vulgar gaze. At length, with the ponderous mass of Ben Wyvis full in view, we reach our journey's end. There are two series of cascades which must be seen separately, for both are not visible from any one point. In the first, the river, after a peaceful and happy childhood, creeps in between two rugged, rocky knolls, and as it does so, finds a wild succession of ugly boulders and out-jutting ledges and obstructing masses in its path. Over these, or under them, or between them, the undaunted stream pours its broken waters, till brown rock and grey ledge and dark pool and yellow cascade meet in a confused medley of colour and form and sound, which sinks down into an inky pool below. Thence again the black waters, with ragged threads of white upon their crawling surface, slink away toward the right behind a bushy spur of rock. In this wild fall and stealthy flight, the river, which came to meet us face to face between the opposing rocks above, has turned abruptly, right in front of us, and crept out of sight to prepare for its second and far grander descent. No one who has an eye to the wild and picturesque will, by uttering any complaint, make true the words of the poet :

" Nature, disturbed,
Is deemed vindictive to have changed her course."

Now we must make a wide circuit and steep descent to a far lower level. Here we cautiously step along a narrow ledge of rough conglomerate covered with heather, ferns, and blaeberries until we arrive right in front of the second—which is the most impressive, series of cascades. How shall I describe what we now behold? We sit or kneel on the brink of a perpendicular rough wall, over which we dare scarcely look; and the great, black, oval-shaped basin between that wall and the cataracts opposite lies some fifty feet below us. The chief and most interesting cascade is right in front of us, and we can scan its course from top to bottom. Up against the western sky is a brown, mossy bank crowned with crested fir trees between whose red, naked stems we can watch the ever-changing light of the declining sun. Beneath that bank is a gravelly scar of yellow and orange on whose over-hanging face some green plants and mountain flowers cling to a precarious life. A little to the left, right up against the scar, stands a sharp, rocky spur, painted over with trailing green, the same behind which we saw the upper waters disappear. Its head is adorned with fresh foliage, and its base sinks imperceptibly into a broad, mural precipice below.

From behind that sharp spur, which the floods have almost made an island, the chastened waters, modest alike in manner and dimensions, creep quietly out into the light, and then! what a fate seems to await their coming! If the weather be fine, and if as a consequence the volume of water be small, we behold a most curious phenomenon. The water takes a spring from the top as if it would drop sheer down without a break into the sullen pool beneath. But no! that is not its fate! It slips instead down the rocky face into a cup-like hollow, and for a space disappears out of sight. But the cup is bottomless, for the stream has bored it through, and the waters pour down the rock again into another dark basin. What looked like the rim of a cup becomes a brown collar tied over the snowy neck of the cascade. Again we look for the waters. There is no visible trace of them on the face of the rock ; but when we carefully observe the surface of another black basin still lower down, we can see by their bubbling and coiling that the adventurous waters have entered it from behind or beneath. In this resting-place also, they tarry for a little time ; then, pouring over the rim, they fall in a broad band of yellow and white, edged with a glittering lace of dewdrops, into the unknown depths of the creeping black pool below.

A little to the left of this singular fall, there is a slanting fissure in the rock, which extends all the way from a gap in the rocky spur above to the surface of the dark basin beneath. In the dry weeks of high summer, a tiny thread of water, all but broken here and there, trickles from top to bottom, while a broad band of blackened rock by its side shows that in stormy weather the thread becomes a long thick white tassel, and deserves the name of cascade on its own account.

If the Aultgraat be in high flood, how different is all this scene ! The upper series of cascades becomes one tremendous broad rush of wriggling, curling, wrestling torrent, out of whose chaotic, foaming surface scarcely an inch of rock dare show itself. From their spring high up between the projecting knolls to the hungry-looking depths of the upper pool, the waters toss up wreath after wreath of gauzy spray to make brilliant rainbows in the sunlight. At the same time the nether fall hides all its mysterious and fantastic features in one breathless, head-long rush of creamy white, while the long slanting fissure almost rivals in volume of water the main body of the cataract. Dashing furiously down with headlong speed, the fevered waters stir and lash the jet black pool into a seething, fermenting, whirling mass of foam. At such a time, the stream—baited into fury, agitated beyond measure—rages down the whole glen, and has not even recovered its temper or natural calm when it plunges into the later sorrows of the Black Rock chasm.

Everything attractive which can be gathered into the highest levels of the picturesque is to be found around these falls. You have mountain and moor, wood and water, cascade and cliff, rocky ridges and flowery banks, sleeping pools and impetuous currents. You behold nature, not tamed and trimmed into squares of grain or root crops, not with her fair face lacerated by roads and railways, but above all rule save that of her own fascinating variety. Of these striking falls and their framework of surrounding scenery, you may well say :

"Nature here
Wanton'd as in her prime and played at will
Her virgin fancies."

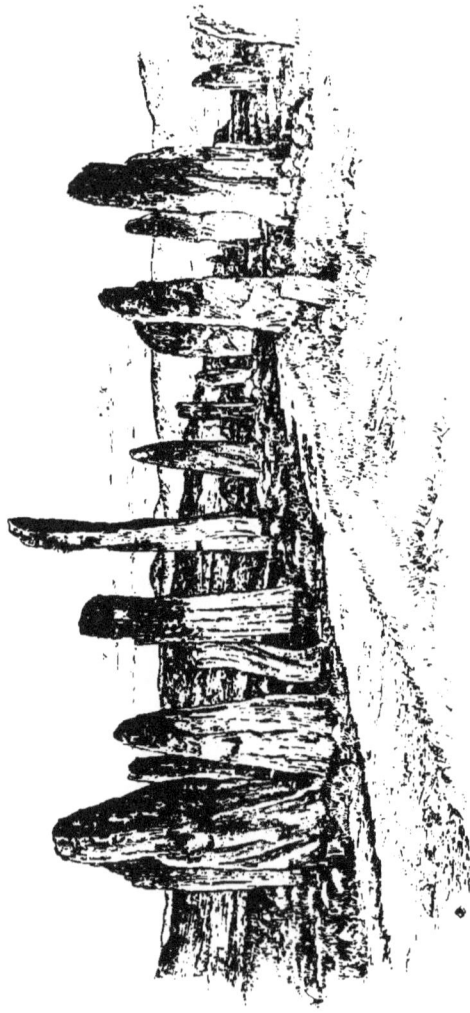

From Photo. by G. W. Wilson.

DRUIDICAL STONES, CALLERNISH, LEWIS.

CHAPTER III.

THE Island of Lewis, the largest of the Hebrides, lies some forty miles off the western shores of Ross and Sutherland, the wide and stormy sound known as the Minch running between. It lies on the Atlantic bosom like a diamond-shaped pendant on a fair lady's breast, but the edges are so indented with deep bays, and long narrow inlets that the coast line must be little less, if not even more, than twenty times the length of the island. At the rough angle on the eastern side there runs out a long peninsula, shaped like a mushroom ; and in the bend where it touches the mainland on the south lie the bay and town of Stornoway. The whole island at one time belonged to the family of Macleods, but passed, about the beginning of the seventeenth century, into the hands of the powerful Mackenzies of Kintail.

On our way to visit "the Lews," as it is often called, we crossed the Minch from Lochinver in a somewhat heavy sea. The waves were breaking constantly over the bow of the steamer, and frequently drenched the bridge also with water. There was nothing to be called either gale or storm, so that there was no danger ; but many of the passengers appeared no less timid than wretched, which is saying a good deal.   Their condition reminded me of an East Coast captain, who was rather a rough customer, and at times very out-spoken, to put it mildly, in his language.   He was a strong, burly man, with a face of deep red colour almost approaching to purple.   On one occasion, during a stiff north-east gale, when heavy seas were sweeping his vessel's decks, and the wild wind howling angrily in the rigging, there was a very timid passenger on board.   This gentleman, who could not be persuaded to go below, stood trembling and shivering on the after part of the bridge, and nervously clutched the rails with his hands.   Once or twice he ventured, timidly but anxiously, to ask the captain if there was any danger, to which that officer always replied that he might keep his mind at rest, there was no danger whatever.   The same enquiry, however, was repeated once too often, for at length the captain turned upon his questioner, and vented his impatience in a stentorian key—

"Now, Sir, I'll tell you what it is, and let this be an end of it.   When you see my face as white like a sheet as your own, you may take it for granted that there may be some danger ; but, not till then."

The traveller, more timid and cowed-looking than ever, made no more inquiries.

Stornoway, the chief, or rather the only, town of the Hebrides, is a lively little sea-port, with signs of activity and prosperity which often surprise strangers.   Picturesque in situation, quaint in many of its aspects, it has become the great centre of the fishing industry on the

West Coast, and the one source of supply for all southern
products and luxuries, including tourists, to the whole
island of Lewis. On the hillside opposite the town, and
looking down upon the harbour, stands Stornoway Castle,
the seat of Lady Matheson, its richly wooded grounds
kept with scrupulous and lavish care. But I must call a
halt in time. If you wish to know the capital city in
more detail, please consult your guide-books, and leave
me to my own scenes and memories.

The general features of the Island of Lewis are few in
number, but well marked and distinctive in character.
The shores are everywhere rocky and rugged, save where,
at wide intervals, they are interrupted by broad bays or
narrow sea lochs, which terminate in green glens among
the hills. The middle and northern districts are for the
most part great stretches of flat or undulating moorland, dotted all over with hundreds of little lochs and
tarns, into which no burns tumble, and out of which
no rivers flow. Yet how pretty these flat saucers of rain-
water are—scores and scores of them glistening in the sunshine like silver ornaments laid out to view upon a russet
ground. In the south and south-west, the mountains are
thickly studded and lofty, but long, twisting arms of the
sea boldly creep in between them, and almost meet from
opposite sides of the island. Many of these inlets taper
away to narrow points, which are hidden in deep valleys
eight or ten miles from the open sea. So many are the
fresh-water lochs and the insinuating strips of the ocean,
that, in bird's eye view, the whole island must resemble
a diamond window with its countless rain-drops darting

one into the other at the beginning of a shower. The hill-tops are singularly wild and bare, scarce a tinge of green relieving the yellow masses of rock and stone ; but in the valleys there are many choice spots of sweet verdure and beauty. An old writer compares the island to a cap with a gold band around it—the latter term denoting the cultivated spots which lie in the valleys, or by the shores. The simile is not a happy one, but may be allowed to pass if we suppose the cap to be second-hand, and much the worse for wear, because then we can account for the many ragged gaps in the band of gold.

The people of Lewis are not purely Celtic as to blood and character. In the north of the island especially there are many evidences of the Norse element both in the people and their ways, and in the names of places as well. There are strong affinities between the natives there and the Scandinavian settlers of Orkney and Shetland ; and no wonder,—the reason is not very far to seek. The frequent invasions and settlements of the Vikings in the days of old have left indelible marks upon the men and the scenery of the Butt of Lewis. It is not possible, however, in all cases, to separate what is Celtic from what is Norse. The two elements have long ago become largely fused into one another ; the habits of the two races have grown together ; and Gaelic, whatever once may have been, is now the common language of all. It has always been a pet idea with me, that this admixture of Celtic and Scandinavian blood should and will produce, if social and economic conditions admitted of fair play, as fine a race of men, physically, intellectually, and morally, as any which has ever lived upon earth. This view I venture to put in type, *pace* the Saxon-born southerner. It will be no surprise to me if some day or other, even if I should not live to see it, "the Lews" sends out a man of front rank into the world. To ask me to mention or disclose in what particular line this Lewsman will excel and rise into wide fame, is neither fair nor kind; it is going too far. Meantime we must be content with what we find; and I now offer some memories and musings, chiefly relating to the island, which have, at least, the merit of variety.

A few days after our arrival, we left Stornoway by the north road, which skirts the inmost recess of the Broad Bay, and then breaks—about a mile further on—into a wide fork. To the left lies the highway to Barvas, a township some twelve miles off over a crawling, winding, moorland road on which not more than one or two houses are to be seen. Yet how much there is for which to be thankful! It seems hardly credible, but is a fact nevertheless, that fifty years ago, though there were some roads, there was not a single bridge in the island. If people would cross streams, either on business or to escape the fairies, they must ford them on foot, or on horseback, or on man-back. It is even said—surely by some ill-natured libeller of the weaker sex, that women carried men—husbands, brothers, even lovers—across the fords upon their backs. These happy days are now long gone by; and yellow streaks of road creep here and there all over the island.

At the angle of departure, we chose the route to the

right, keeping nearer the coast line, and after a long walk reached a typical Lewis village.

Let me first sketch the outward features of a single dwelling. The walls of a cottage belonging to a crofter or fisherman are usually about six feet high or little more. They have an outer and inner face built of rough stones all sizes and shapes, the space between filled with earth or rubbish. On the top of this wall, which is often four feet thick and more, there are built up layers of turf which form a broad ledge all round the base of the roof, like the rim of a strong boot along the edge of the upper. This flat wall-top, covered with grass and weeds, is a promenade and feeding ground for the sheep and poultry, and often a look-out for women who expect husbands or brothers home from sea. The roof proper starts from the inner edge of the wall head. The rafters are often few and thin, because all wood for such purposes must be imported from the mainland and is therefore high in price. After the framework is up, layers of turf are laid upon the beams, and over these again a thick coating of grey thatch. To make all tight and fast, straw ropes are thrown over the rounded ridge, and their ends whipped firmly round large stones which serve and are known as *anchors*, to moor the roof in a storm. If anything more be needed, a harrow thrown over a damaged corner may check further mischief for a time. Some of the houses are very short and small; but others are long and roomy. All appear diminutive and squat-looking, so much so that an old writer of playful humour remarks that one could put his hand down the smoke-

hole in the roof and unlatch the door. This is a quiet
and harmless joke, no doubt; but if anyone were foolish
enough to make the attempt, the result might be serious
—for him. I say this, because we have a remarkable
warning on record, though it be several centuries old.
A travelling shoemaker came on a Sabbath night to a
covenanter's dwelling. He had been promised a week's
work in the family, and intended to begin betimes on
Monday morning. Afraid of being reproved for travelling on the day of rest, he slipped secretly up to a loft
above the kitchen. Through a wide square hole in the
floor of this upper chamber, the smoke from the central
fire below found its way upwards to the aperture in the
roof, and so to the open air. Tired with his journey,
Birsy, for that was his name, fell fast asleep. His
awaking was rude and alarming, and took place while
the household were at family worship. First an awl,
then a broad-bladed knife, fell on to the hearth below,
causing no little flutter; and finally the cobbler himself
toppled over and descended with a blinding splutter into
the fire around which the family were gathered. What
a wide-spread scattering of ashes was there! What a
panic and stampede among human kind, great and small,
old and young alike! Therefore I cordially commend
the lesson to thieves and other fools in Lewis. Let
them beware. The descent from the canless vent in the
roof to the fire on the hearth below is straight as an
arrow, and sure to lead to shame.

A Lewis village is usually a cluster of closely-packed
dwellings, which from a height or from a distance look

like groups of grey mole-hills in a patch of rough grass. Only narrow causeways, always rough and often very filthy, separate wall from wall or gable from gable. At some places a few cottages straggle along the roadside, while here and there, on moorland or shore, a few stand apart and alone. One of these latter we visited on the day already mentioned; why and how, it is now my duty to tell.

After attempting some sketching in the intervals between showers, and visiting a small church and a few dwellings near by, we turned our steps homewards, that is, towards Stornoway. It was high time, for heavy swollen clouds from the far west were creeping toward us over hill and moor, dropping here and there a grey-blue band of soaking rain upon the earth. At length a gusty wind and pitiless shower drove us for shelter to a low mean-looking hovel which we took for a byre, and in its deep-set doorway we crouched from the blast. After a little we were greatly surprised to hear the sound of voices within, and by and by an old woman, coming to the door, courteously beckoned us to enter and rest for a while. In my best Gaelic I tried to thank her, and we accepted the invitation. The interior was of the type most common in Lewis, and deserves a few words of description. The house was divided into three distinct compartments. The door by which we entered opened into the byre, where there were two or three stalls for cows on the gable end, and in front of these the usual gutter with its usual contents. Then came two dwarf walls some five or six feet high, with an open-

ing between them, but no door to fill it. This was the
entrance to the central and most important division of
the dwelling—the scene of all the active indoor life of
the inmates. On a raised hearth in the centre of the
floor burned a merry, kindly-looking peat fire with its
soft fringe of white and orange ashes. On either side,
against the opposite walls, were broad benches, which
could easily accommodate a large family and one or two
visitors besides. Beyond this compartment again, was
the door—really a door this time—of the spare or best
room, a small chamber with a mahogany table, box
beds, and one or two chests painted in green and red.
The smoke of the peat fire in the middle division rose
reluctantly upward, and was drawn out by a wide
aperture on the ridge of the roof, while, as part of the
same arrangement, another hole just over the wall-head
in a far corner, created as much draught as was needed.
If the current of air became too strong, a wisp of straw
stuffed into the said hole prevented excessive ventilation.
One custom, peculiar, so far as I have heard, to the Lews,
must here be mentioned. The crofters and fishermen
take the thatch and turf off the roofs of their houses
every year or two and use them for manure, for which
purpose they are said to be most valuable. No wonder,
therefore, that the inmates are rather pleased than otherwise to have their roofs blackened and saturated with
peat smoke, which supplies the most valuable ingredients
in the fertilising process. Within doors in a Lewis
dwelling, the prevailing atmosphere is a misty blue, light
in colour but dense in quality, which for a time is very

trying to the eyes of strangers. Such are many homes which have been abodes of genuine piety, and from which have gone forth bands of the hardiest sailors and bravest soldiers of which our country can boast.

The inmates of the cottage were three in number—the kindly old woman who asked us to enter; her daughter, a cheerful, young wife, whose husband was a mechanic in Stornoway; and last, but not least important, an infant child, buried among clothes in a fish creel, for want of a better cradle. The younger mother told us she was merely on a visit to "grannie," who wanted to see and dote over her grandson. We were by no means inquisitive, and neither were they; yet, little by little, we learnt a good deal about each other. The old woman, knowing nothing but Gaelic, spoke only to or through her daughter; but if that obstacle could have been removed, she would have displayed, I believe, very remarkable conversational powers. From time to time I stepped out to the door to see if there was any blue sky visible, but the watery gusts were still sweeping by with undiminished fury and frequency. Meantime, without any interruption to our talk, the young woman quietly infused tea, and set it on the hearth, drew cups and saucers from a trunk in the inner room, and handed to each of us large sea biscuits, each one of which bore its burden of excellent cheese. Our repast was both " grateful and comforting," and we shall none of us forget one of its accompaniments. The grandmother had by this time found out that I understood some portions of the Gaelic conversation which passed between herself

and her daughter. From that moment many of her remarks were intended for my special benefit, but I was
careful to keep well within my depth in reply. At
length, without asking for it, we were afforded the rich
treat, which adds, to us at least, so much interest to the
memory of our visit. The old woman, when her daughter
was busy, had lifted the little child from its strange crib,
and laid him on her lap. Then, bending her keen, dark
eyes and unkempt hair over his chubby face, she rocked
her body to and fro, and crooned the plaintive Æolian
strains of some ancient Gaelic air. Both in itself and in
its harmony of circumstances, that weird lullaby remains
to us a precious and fascinating memory. Much rather
should I prefer to hear it again than to sit through half
the concerts and operas and classical music of a London
season. Of course, that confession is most heretical, and
shows what many people will call a low level of taste.
So be it ; think so if you will. At once I take my stand
in this matter by the side of my old teacher, Professor
Blackie, and for the present am content to fling at your
heads the old adage, *diversos diversa juvant.* By-and-
by the rain ceased, and we resumed our long tramp to
the town. All the details of our parting with the
inmates of the cottage are not for the public at large.
We shall never forget the homely and natural kindness
with which we were welcomed and entertained.

Allow me here a wide digression on the subject of
language, and of the many blunders which have been
made by Celts and Saxons alike when away from their
respective homes. We shall take the Saxon first, and

E

give the natives of the Highlands the first of the laugh.

My knowledge of Gaelic—once fair for one who is no Celt—is now very slight indeed. I used to be told, "They'll no sell you in it," but I fear that now, if the attempt were made without much ostentation, the bargain might be struck before I was aware. Therefore, I seldom attempt to use the language unless for a little sport or in necessity. Yet my canon for learning a strange tongue is entirely different from that system of caution, and is indeed very simple. Study grammar, write exercises, read extracts of books—do these certainly; but above all, speak, speak, speak, every chance you can get, and no matter how many blunders you may make. By such a method, you will gain ever so much daily, and lose nothing except, perhaps, a little stupid pride. But that advice is only for private use. How many men have made, and daily make, asses of themselves by venturing to speak publicly in a language which they have not mastered. Let me give you a few rather amusing instances. Whether they are all, or even most of them, from the Lews or no, I cannot tell; but most of them are from the pulpit, which ought to be quite as good a source.

In a certain rural parish in the north, there lived and laboured an excellent Christian minister, who had acquired a knowledge of Gaelic, because he earnestly desired to preach to Highlanders in their native tongue. It will be matter of surprise to no one that, during the early years of his ministry especially, he made frequent, and often grotesque, blunders. The following is one speci-

men out of very many which have been current. It was
a warm, bright summer day, and the doors of the church
at the further end from the pulpit were thrown wide open
to admit a current of air from without. At one passage
of his discourse, which seems to have been of a hortatory
nature, the minister meant to convey the earnest counsel,
" Be up and doing ; spring is at the door," and he
thought he had said so as correctly as fervently. Unfortunately, what reached the ears of his Gaelic audience
was this : " Be up and doing ; there's a colt at the door."
At once four hundred heads were turned toward the open
door to see the animal enter. The colt, however, never
appeared ; and I question if the good old man ever knew
of the error he had committed. The words " spring "
and " colt " in Gaelic are closely similar in sound.

Another preacher who had sought and found a quiet
retreat in the remote Highlands for the very purpose of
acquiring the language, fell into a similar mistake. He
had travelled some distance to make a call, and on arriving at the house of some friends, astonished them by
declaring, " Tha tri raidhean f'on ah' fhàg sinn," which
is, being interpreted, " I left my own house three quarters of a year ago." Whether he was asked to narrate
the story of his wanderings in the interval, we are not
told; perhaps an amused smile on the faces of his friends
might induce him to suspect that something was wrong.
Probably he would ere long be awakened to the fact
that there is a difference, which exists even in Gaelic,
between a year and an hour.

Another case was more unfortunate, because, as in the

first, the blunder was made in public. Towards the close
of the service, a minister proceeded to make some intima-
tions from the pulpit. Among others, he intended to
announce that on the following Lord's Day there would
be a collection for the poor of the congregation. But,
alas, for him! he forgot how nearly alike in sound are
the words "bochd," signifying poor, and "boc," which
means a buck. The word he uttered was the latter instead of the former, so that he startled his audience by
solemnly intimating a collection for *the bucks* of the
congregation! We can easily understand to what inquiries this interesting call to benevolence might give
rise, especially among the young ladies. Who were these
bucks? Were they many in number? Why were con-
tributions asked on their behalf? Were they in poverty
or in debt, or in both together? Had extravagance in
costume or luxury in living brought them into straits?
We have, unfortunately, no answer to any of these questions, nor have we any record of the amount of the collection when it came off. It would be interesting to know
how far so touching an appeal for a deserving class had
reached the hearts of the people.

One instance more let me offer of the ignorance and
rash folly of the Saxon when he attempts to air himself
in the earliest and greatest of all languages. In this
case, the minister was impressing upon his audience their
needy and lost condition in a spiritual sense. He meant
to enforce upon them the conviction that they were
"peacaich thruagh chaillte," that is, poor lost sinners.
His actual words were somewhat similar in sound, but

widely different in meaning. Imagine the feelings of his
hearers when he called them "picich chruaidh shaillte,"
that is, *hard, salted saith*, the saith being a coarse, deep-
sea fish, often caught and cured in the western and
northern isles. It is much to be feared that both mind
and conscience among his hearers would refuse assent to
such a description—even coming *ex cathedrá*—and
might even resent it as an insult. Perhaps it is still
more likely that the announcement was received in quite
another spirit. The Highlanders, like the French, are
very indulgent toward foreigners who blunder in their
language. Probably the congregation heard their
minister expose his ignorance with a kindly pity flitting
in smiles from face to face.

Now, being myself a Norseman in blood and sympathies, I should like to hold the scales evenly between
Saxon and Celt. Therefore my digression as to Gaelic
must lead to another. Possibly some ardent Celts may
store up some of the above blunders in memory, and
upon occasion fling them gleefully in the face of the
Saxon. We must, therefore, provide the latter with a
few pebbles to sling back. Not too abruptly, however,
must we approach the delicate subject of Highland
frailty. If I handle it too roughly, I shall pay for it
next time I visit the north.

The Lewis people are deeply attached to their native
island. Local patriotism burns strongly and steadily in
their bosoms. They are reluctant to leave the scenes of
their birth and youth, and fain—even if they have
wandered to far-off lands—to return again to the island

which has never ceased to be home. It was an American,
but it might well have been a Lewsman, who wrote—

> " Me whom the city holds, whose feet
> Have worn its stony highways,
> Familiar with its loneliest street,
> Its ways were never my ways—
> My cradle was beside the sea,
> And there, I hope, my grave will be."

Yet many leave the island, as they do other parts of the
west and north, to better their condition or status in life.
Among this class perhaps the most interesting are the
youths who go south to our Universities, in order to study
for one or other of the learned professions. Through what
a hard struggle has many a Highland student fought and
won his way ! All honour to his dauntless perseverance
and courage ! Yet there are few such men in whose
careers there have not been one or two strange or
amusing episodes. They know the English language
sometimes very imperfectly ; and the conditions and
habits of city life often land them in trouble.

Well do I remember the case of one such student—I
shall not say where he came from—with whom I had a
slight acquaintance at college. He had taught a school
in the north for many years, and was well advanced in
middle life when he came to Edinburgh. After passing
through the Arts classes, he proposed to study for the
Church. In order to do this he must needs be examined
by his local Presbytery. One incident in that process is
worthy of mention. A well-known and excellent
minister was appointed to ask him some questions in
mathematics. The first of these came off as follows :

" Well, Mr F., let us begin with what is very simple. Would you be so kind as tell me,—What is a point ? " The student looks bashful, and is silent. He must be spurred up a bit.

" Come away, Mr F., I'm sure that's very easy. What is a point ? " The student begins to feel that he must make some reply, so he deems it wise policy to win, if he can, the good graces of his examiner. Accordingly, with an insinuating smile, he suggests—

" Oh, Mr G., ye ken yersel ; ye ken fine yersel."

" Well," replied the minister, " perhaps I do ; but that's not *the* point. What I want is that *you* should tell *me.* Come away, What is a point ? "

The poor student feels that the question must now be fairly faced ; he can temporise no longer. Accordingly, after a prolonged nervous application of his fingers to the crown of his head, he dropped his hand, bobbed his fore-finger sharply on the table, and with an air of conscious triumph, exclaimed,

" A dabbie like that ; jist a dabbie like that."

We can guess the general character of the questions and answers which followed.

The story of one of Mr F.'s great difficulties in a theo-logical class is still a lively tradition in student circles. One of the professors was examining orally—the subject being a somewhat unusual one, the Jewish marriage law. Mr F. was called, at once stood upon his feet, and prepared to receive cavalry. He made, however, but a poor stand. At every question put—for he could answer none of them—Mr F. nudged the student next to him

with his elbow, and whispered sideways, " Tell me, man,
tell me." This was repeated several times, and did
indeed produce one or two bungling answers. At length
the professor saw that the student was utterly lost in the
depths. With the kindly intention of restoring him to
terra firma, he thus addressed the trembling sufferer
with an encouraging smile—

" Well, Mr F., perhaps you can answer this one. Are
you married yourself?"

So utterly bewildered was the student that he did not
even catch the question, so he nudged his neighbour as
vigorously as ever with,

" Tell me, man, tell me."

In very wantonness of mischief the other whispered
back, " Say yes," and his counsel was taken without a
word of question.

" Yes, sir," said Mr F. timidly and modestly ; and the
very walls resounded with the strong laughter of the
Professor and his class. After a few moments Mr F.
recovered himself. He believed he had for once made a
great hit ; and therefore he contributed a broad, benevolent smile to the merriment. It was only at the end
of the class hour that he understood what had taken
place.

Another such case arose from sheer ignorance of polite
or scrupulous habits. A Highland student was invited
to breakfast at one of the Professor's houses, and happened to be seated near the hostess at table. His plate
was supplied with fish ; and, as he ate, he pitched fragments of bone over his shoulder, and they alighted on

the carpet behind. The lady ventured to remonstrate once and again,

"Just leave the bones on your plate, Mr M.; don't trouble to throw them away."

A second and third time the offence was repeated, and the lady grew more importunate.

"Leave them on your plate, Mr M., please don't trouble to throw them away."

All unconscious of the cause of her anxiety, the student finally silenced her by replying,

"It's no trouble, ma'am; no trouble at all."

The summary process went on until the plate was cleared. The lady was pitiful, the student happy and unruffled. He had seldom, perhaps, enjoyed a better breakfast up to that hour; he has had very many as good or better at his own table in subsequent years.

During our stay on the island we spent the best part of at least one whole day upon the moors. Taking a light luncheon with us, and making an early start, we chose the route through the well-kept grounds and rich woods of Stornoway Castle. What a contrast do these full-grown trees, and vigorous shrubs, and brilliant flower-beds present to the general character of the scenery around! They quite remind one of Mr Hanbury's famous grounds at Mortola on the Riviera, where human skill and Mediterranean sunshine have converted a steep, stony hillside into a Paradise of rich verdure and shady foliage. Here in the grounds of the Lewis Castle, skill and money have not been spared, and the result is wonderful; but, alas! the marvellous sunshine is wanting. Once

through the woods we came upon the banks of the
Creid, or Creed, which falls into the Bay of Stornoway.
Its dancing waters rushed by as if in their haste they
had no time even to greet us.   By and by, we came out
upon the road, which had made a wide circuit round the
Castle policies ; and very soon we left behind all sight of
either houses or trees.   At a distance of less than three
miles from the town, there is no trace or evidence of
human life to be found save the road on which we walk,
and here and there a deep cutting of peat.   Round and
round on every hand there lies a dreary dead expanse of
flat moorland—its long, low undulations thickly sprinkled
over with little lochs and tarns.   Nothing bounds it
save its own level horizon, except to the far west and
south, where a long range of hills with many rounded
peaks rises like a rugged Galloway dyke against the sky.
The moor itself is thickly covered with banks and tufts
of heather, among which are scattered plants of bog
myrtle, and white tassels of cotton-grass like snow-
flakes which have wandered one by one from a passing
shower.   As to feathered fowl there was scarce the flutter
of a wing.   Only once that day, as we sat sketching a
brown loch with the mountain range as a distant back-
ground, a water fowl flew over the dark brown mirror,
scratching its smooth surface with its wing-tips, and
then sinking out of view in the motley heather.   To
many, that far-stretching plateau, without tree or stream
or flower, might, notwithstanding the sunshine, seem
dreary even to desolation ; but it had a charm and even
fascination of its own.   In its unbroken repose beneath

the sunlight; in its fulness and warmth of colour; in its
wealth of waters, like bright coins upon its bosom; in
its long undulations like far-off Atlantic rollers; and in
its western fence of hill tops, which show in brilliant
pink at the setting of the sun, the moorland has beauty
under its tameness, and variety under its sombre surface.
What gorgeous sunsets have been mirrored in these flat
sheets of water! What conflicts of quivering lights has
the belated traveller seen in that northern sky! Round
about these tarns have the sportive fairies chased one
another, and when wearied have gathered in a circle to
sing the happy chorus:

"By the moon we sport and play;
With the night begins our day;
As we dance, the dew doth fall;
Trip it, little urchins all,
Lightly as the nimble bee,
Two by two, and three by three,
And about go we, and about go we."

During that very day on which we visited the moor
of Arnish, we had a most satisfying experience of the one
incurable misery of the Lews. The atmosphere was per-
vaded with that peculiar luminosity, which often ac-
companies calm and heat, and as a consequence we were
assailed from morning till night by multitudinous clouds
of tiny midges. The common house fly, as we all know,
displays much activity and bravery when you lie down
to steal an after-dinner nap; but for persistency and
brazen impudence, he must hide his diminished head in
presence of the midges. It is notoriously very difficult
to estimate numbers. Even the most cautious and

experienced are apt to form too high an estimate of a crowd. On the Arnish road we had the same difficulty to face; for we had to deal with a largely attended public meeting, and the crowds came and went continually. Still, I do not hesitate to say, that within a radius of say ten yards round about us, the number of the midges was at least equal to the present population of the Chinese Empire, whatever that may be. How many we slew with our hands; how many we swallowed; how many committed suicide before our eyes on our oil canvasses, it is impossible to say; but one strange fact impressed us greatly. As the hours went by, we could detect no diminution whatever, not even of a single midge, in the myriad hosts of our assailants. Perhaps travellers who come after us may be able to confirm this experience by their own.

At this point I am tempted to make a confession in order to follow it up with an explanation regarding the midges. I suppose every young man of average ability or less has been tempted once at least to " commit poetry," though he generally hides his sin. Once at least in my early days, I perpetrated a few verses, which start to memory in connection with the midges. Under a certain influence, which I shall not name or define, I promised to give up smoking for several months. That same night I sat down and wrote " An Address to his Divorced Spouse by a Disconsolate Widower "—my pipe being the spouse, and I the disconsolate. Fortunately, I can only remember the first and last two verses; but here they are—

"My darling pipe ! a long adieu !
No more, alas ! 'twixt me and you
    The happy times of yore ;
The sweet acquaintanceship we had,
The many hours you made me glad,
    Are gone for evermore.

    *   *   *   *

"Farewell, the deep and dreamy joy,
Farewell, the calm without alloy,
    Which thou wert wont to bring !
With no regret to rack my heart,
With no remorse from thee I part,
    And o'er thy grave will sing !

"A long farewell ! a glad farewell !
Bravely I tear away the spell
    Around my heart that grew.
Thou horrid weed ! avaunt with speed
So purely vile, so full of guile,
    A long, a last adieu !"

I have only quoted these verses to confess that after all it was not a "long," neither was it a "last," adieu ; and for that I was duly and truly thankful on the "day of the midges." Nothing but clouds of tobacco smoke cooled their ardour for an instant, and I was very happy indeed that I had broken the above poetical vows into a thousand shivers many a long day before. Even ladies, in such a time of distress, do not object to have a puff or two in their very faces. So true is the old adage, that circumstances alter cases.

As I have alluded to one source of misery in Lewis, I may also mention another, not altogether wanting, as my readers will remember, in the region of Loch Duich. Generally speaking, you need not trouble to take

umbrellas to the island, and I shall tell you why.
To put the matter in few words, it is this : if it's fair
in Lewis, it's fair ; if it rains, it rains. This may seem
very simple, and even trite ; but many pregnant truths
are so. If it's fair, you need no umbrella ; if it rains, no
umbrella yet invented will keep you dry, so you had better
stay indoors. Even a London bus-driver, with his red
mushroom overhead, would be soaked to the skin in
rather less than ten minutes. But all has not yet been
told. Probably the climate is, on the whole, not much
different from what it used to be, say, fifty years ago. A
worthy clergyman tells us that it was then very damp.
Here are his very words : " The dampness of the air is such
that, in rooms wherein fires are not constantly kept, the
walls emit a hoary down of a brinish taste, resembling
pounded saltpetre when brushed off. The climate is an
enemy to polished iron and to books. Fire-irons rust in
the space of twenty-four hours without constant fire; and
books are covered with a greyish-yellow mould, unless
frequently wiped." How great is the temptation to
moralise which these words present ! One reflection only
shall I put on record. What a mercy for him that Beau
Brummel never lived in Stornoway ! You remember
how he complained that he had caught a cold by sleeping one night in the same room with a damp stranger.
In what condition would he be found, if alive at all,
after a night among books and fire-irons in the Island of
Lewis ?

Another reflection, and then we may pass from this
theme. How strong and hardy must the natives them-

selves be to reach manhood and womanhood under such
conditions! This exceptional vigour and vitality explains
many things. No wonder, for example, that Birt, who
visited the Highlands in 1725, speaks of seeing dark
patches, each of something like human shape, among the
wreaths of snow. They were simply the spots where
the clansmen had lain over night. No wonder, also,
that they have shown such endurance and prowess in
war. From my boyish days I have been amazed, many
a time and oft, at a certain statement in an old ballad-
song, which describes the battle of Harlaw in 1411. It
was a desperate and prolonged conflict between Highlanders and Royal troops, in which the former were
undoubtedly victorious at the end. What I want you
to note, however, is the duration of the battle, for, so far
as I am aware, it is without a parallel in history—

> " This fecht began on Monanday
>   By risin' o' the sun ;
> An' on Saturday at twal o'clock,
>   Ye'd scarce ken wha wud wun."

Think of the "staying powers" there displayed! Since
I have visited Lewis, and made acquaintance with midges
and damp, I have ceased to wonder at the protracted
struggle, or at the final triumph of the western islanders.

It may be interesting at this point to offer some
remarks as to ways of courtship and customs of marriage
in some of the remoter parts of Lewis. I have said
courtship, but I daresay many will be disposed to say
that what I am to describe does not deserve that inter-

esting name. In outlying districts of the island, marriages do not always arise from love, nor are they preceded by long or sweetly - protracted advances on the part of the young man toward the young lady. The whole matter is, to a large extent, one of business or *convenance.* It hinges very much on the all-important question whether the lady is an adept in handling and bearing the " creel." This is of course due to the fact that the said article plays an active part in many operations of daily life. It is used to carry out to the fields the piled-up manure-heap of the byre—an annual piece of work ; to carry loads of peats from the moors ; to bring great burdens of seaweed from the shore ; to convey food to the cattle in the *airidh,* or green shealing among the hills ; and for many other purposes besides. Hence arises the high value set upon the ability to work the creel. A young man's courtship very often originates with his parents. An elderly man on some suitable occasion addresses his spouse after this fashion (in Gaelic of course, but I give the substance in English) :

" Well, Maggie, you have always been a good and faithful wife to me. I am afraid, however, that you are not so strong as you once were. Your diligence and industry with the creel have broken down your strength. You deserve some measure of relief and rest. We must ask our son Donald to get married, and his wife will take the heavy burdens off your shoulders."

Then the guidman and his wife discuss over the fire what fair buxom maiden would be a suitable bride for

the excellent young man Donald. Half the robust girls
of the neighbourhood pass in review before their minds.
By-and-bye Donald himself is informed of his parents'
ideas; and whatever his personal feelings may be, he
considers it to be his duty to exercise self-denial, and to
please his father and mother. The next step is to order
a bottle of whisky from Stornoway; and several days
may elapse before its arrival. When the liquor has
come, the old man and his son wend their way to the
dwelling of the young woman who is first-favourite. The
bottle is stowed away out of sight. For a time they
chat and gossip pleasantly with the family, and by-and-
bye the purpose of their visit is disclosed. The girl's
parents may be well pleased, perhaps even flattered ; but
she herself may be coy and reluctant. Perhaps the proposal has come upon her as a sudden surprise, and she
does not like frankly to say, even to her mother, that she
would require a few days to think the matter over. If
any signs of hesitation thus appear, Donald and his father
consider that their proposal is rejected, and at once rise
to leave the house. They wish the inmates good-night,
and enjoy a little malicious satisfaction in thinking how
sorry the poor folks will be at the loss of a possible dram.
Once outside, the father and son hold a hurried consulta-
tion, and soon decide to visit another dwelling. On this
second occasion also some unpropitious element from the
side of parents or daughter may mar the success of their
quest. Once more they bid a disappointed farewell, and
leave the house behind. One might imagine that these
failures would damp their spirits, and induce them to

F

turn their steps homewards ; but it is not so. The dauntless bravery which has served the old man in good stead
during many a difficulty and danger at sea, does not fail
him in present straits.   Addressing his son, who is
perhaps a little dejected, he says,

"Donald, lad, we must not let this business fall
to the ground. We left home for a special purpose, and
we must not return to confess ourselves beaten. Come
along with me to Neil M'Leod's house. Mary is the
flower of his family, and if she consents, you, Donald,
will get a good wife, and your mother a splendid helper
for the field and the moss and the cattle."

This time their fond hopes are realised. Mary had
fled when she discovered their errand ; but her mother
draws her from her hiding-place. The young lady's
scruples are overcome by maternal persuasions, and she
consents to have Donald as her husband. Then at last
the bottle is produced, and amid much cordial good
cheer arrangements are made for an early wedding.

The marriage day is a great occasion.   Omitting the
mere ceremony, let me mention some other features of
the gathering. There are gradations of honour and of
treatment among the company. If there is a room-end
in the house, that contains the inner and upper circle.
Among these select guests may be numbered a few of the
elders of the kirk, the schoolmaster, if he is popular, and
those friends who have come from greatest distances. The
table is adorned with plates, forks, and knives, which
have been borrowed for the occasion. Here, too, among
other specialties, are some loaves of bread and a stack

of broad barley scones. In this room also is deposited
the jar of whisky, which is under the absolute control of
the master of ceremonies. It is kept in the bed, and is
guarded by two or three persons, who sit upon the edge
of the coverlet. Out of the jar there is poured a sufficient
quantity of the pure stuff for the wants of the favoured
company in this best room. Then the jar is filled up
with water, perhaps from some dirty pool near the house.
Thus replenished, it is sent, with much show of liberality,
to those outside the select circle. A second party is
gathered in the common room or kitchen, in the centre
of which the peat fire is burning gloriously. Under a
smoky canopy of blue, the guests arrange themselves
around the walls. They are provided with bowls or other
convenient vessels of a miscellaneous kind out of which
to sup their food. There are, of course, large piles of
barley scones, while the chief delicacy in this compartment is a substantial quantity of beef cut up into minute
fragments of various shapes, as if intended for a dish of
hash. This *pièce de resistance* is committed to the care
of young women, who dig their fingers into the masses
of meat, and distribute them here and there in handfuls,
keeping up all the while a running fire of joke and
banter with the lads of the company. Still lower as to
the degree of attention paid to them, are a third class,
who dare not intrude upon the other two, but are allowed
to shift as best they can for themselves. They may locate
themselves in the barn ; or, if there be no barn, on the
manure-heap between the kitchen and the cows, and in
either case are well content. They get food of a quality

superior to any they indulge in at home, and even the adulterated whisky is to them quite a luxury.

Even on these high occasions, instrumental music is seldom employed, being accounted sinful in no ordinary degree. This is largely due to the influence of one popular preacher, who a generation ago denounced and resisted the practice. Even to this day, tender consciences are afraid to allow or countenance the use of the fiddle or bagpipe at marriage festivities. The guests have dancing, however, and a pleasant musical accompaniment as well. The young girls sing songs, usually duets, of native composition, and these are set to tunes which suit the various steps of the lively exercise. By many the effect is thought quite equal to the strains of the fiddle. I have heard of a young man of excellent moral character, who could play the concertina and tin whistle, and was, therefore, much in request at weddings. Even he and his instruments were, however, condemned by the "straitest sect," and fell into disrepute. Not even in the west of Lewis can these prejudices and absurdities live much longer.

Let me add one word more to connect the beginning with the end of this matrimonial theme. In journals and magazines there have been lively discussions of late years on the question, Is Marriage a failure? The people of Lewis make an important contribution to the controversy. They offer a practical test, which they themselves apply; but, alas! only to one sex. Public judgment on the merits of a wife is entirely suspended

until after the birth of her first child. If within a week
from that event she is able to handle and bear the creel
like any of her neighbours, then the husband is congratu-
lated, for his marriage is no failure. If she fails to come
up to the creel standard within the allotted time, then
the man becomes an object of pity and condolence ; he
has made a blunder which can never be repaired. In
the latter case, the words of the poet may be applied—

> " Thus grief still treads upon the heels of pleasure,
> Married in haste, we may repent at leisure."

Before we close this chapter, there are three classes of
the ancient inhabitants of Lewis of whom I should like
to say a few words. I shall do little more than mention
the first two ; but of the third I must speak with some
fulness.

The first class is, of course, the sweet " fairies," or
" guid folk "—fewer far than once they were, and far
more shy of human society. There are many theories to
account for their diminution and retreat, but on these I
have no time to dwell. That they were well known and
often seen in days gone by is attested by the poet who
sings :

> " As when a shepherd of the Hebrid Isles,
> Placed far amid the melancholy main,
> (Whether it be lone fancy him beguiles,
> Or that aërial beings sometimes deign
> To stand embodied, to our senses plain)
> Sees on the naked hill or valley low,
> The whilst in ocean Phœbus dips his wain,
> A vast assembly moving to and fro,
> Then all at once in air dissolves the wondrous show."

Another class, once common enough, but now rarely to be seen, were the Roman Catholic "sisters" or "nuns." Their residences—all now in ruins—are scattered here and there over the island; and are called in Gaelic, "Teagh nan callichan dhu"—"the houses of the old black women." It would appear that their ascetic life is not popular in this thoughtless generation. I should not like to say that the native young ladies go so far as their giddy sister who sang—

"I love to go a-shopping, I love fashionable clothes,
I love music, and dancing, and chatting with the beaux;
So I won't be a nun, no, I shan't be a nun,
I'm so fond of pleasure, that I cannot be a nun;"

but their ideas tend more in that direction than did those of "the old black women." The young ladies of Stornoway take in *The Queen* and the *Lady's Pictorial*, play lawn tennis, and are as sprightly as "The Princess of Thule" herself.

The third class of beings are, strange to say, modern as well as ancient. They are called "Fir Chreig," or the false men. You ask, Who or what are these? They are remarkable standing stones of venerable age, and are named the "false men" because of their fancied resemblance, perhaps in mist or darkness, to men of large stature. They might produce a "false" impression to that effect on certain persons in certain states of mind. But now to sober description.

At Callernish in Loch Roag, on the west coast of Lewis, may be seen a very remarkable group of these standing stones. As specimens of their kind, they are second only to Stonehenge or Stennis in Orkney. They occupy a gentle eminence near by the shore, and are visible from a great distance round about. They have one or two quite unique features, which are worthy of special attention and study. To begin with, these stones are not simply a circle, as many such groups are, but a circle and cross in combination, with some traces of a wide, surrounding trench. The circle consists of large, rough, flat-sided stones, 14 in number, with another central stone, 15 feet high, which has been likened, not inaptly, to a ship's rudder. At the base of the central block were found traces of an old altar or table. This circle of stones lies over the intersection of the arms of a gigantic cross. The long arm, now some 400 feet from end to end, appears once upon a time to have extended as far as 600 feet. It consists of a double row of stones, most of which have fallen, but many are still erect. The shorter or cross arm consists of a single row of stones, and extends to some 200 feet in length. Originally there were probably more than 60 stones, but not more than 50, standing or fallen, can now be found. The blocks are all of gneiss, and their transportation and erection must have been a work of immense labour. Stately and sad, lonely, yet defiant, they stand in rank on that bare knoll, whose base is washed by Atlantic waves.

There is little doubt that these standing stones are a monument of the ancient Druids. These were the priestly caste among the old Gauls and Britons, and taught a religion in which the immortality of the soul and human dependence were prominent elements. But

the Druids were not only priests ; they were philosophers,
holding kindred views to those of Pythagoras ; scientists,
poring deeply into the mysteries of astronomy, geography,
and other branches of learning ; and judges, expounding,
administering, and enforcing the law.   Groves of oak
were their favourite retreats, and they held the misletoe
in peculiar veneration, as an image of man whose life
is wholly dependent on that of Another stronger than
himself.   Whenever that plant was found, a priest,
dressed in white robes, cut it off with a golden knife,
and two bulls were sacrificed on the occasion.   The
chief priest, whose office was not hereditary but elec-
tive, exercised supreme authority for life ; and those
who sought admission to the order must pass through a
novitiate of twenty years.   The ponderous megalithic
remains, which we now see in France and Britain, show
their skill in mechanical art, and raise many questions as
to the design and use of such erections.   To me at least
it seems most likely that these groups of stones served
many and varied ends.   They may have been used for
worship, for instruction, for courts of justice, and even
for the settlement of public questions.   In any case they
are impressive monuments of a far past age, and of a
remarkable order of men.

We left the island of Lewis with real regret.   There
was much to be seen for which we found no time ; and
many known spots among which we would fain have
lingered.   When the hour of departure came, we found
that the island and its people had taken a firmer hold of
our interest and sympathies than we at first suspected.

This was by no means a unique or rare experience, for young men and maidens are said to have felt it when about to part.

> " How oft—if, at the court of love,
> Concealment is the fashion,
> When ' How d'ye do ' has failed to move,
> ' Good-bye ' reveals the passion."

CHAPTER IV.

More than five and twenty years ago, my college friend Ian and I projected for ourselves a summer tour round the north-west and north of Scotland. The district was not entirely unknown to us, but we wished to explore it more thoroughly, and with that end in view we resolved to go on foot. We met at Golspie; spent the night at the picturesquely-situated hotel near Dunrobin Castle, and began our tramp together next morning.

The advantages of walking above all other methods of enjoying the beauties and glories of nature are well known and, I suppose, generally admitted. No doubt, in the case of a tour on foot, you may suffer from occasional fatigue; you may be covered with dust up to the knees, or soaked with rain through all garments, outer and inner alike; you may spend weeks among mountains and valleys through which a demon express might run in a few hours; and your modest speed lays you open to the companionship of clouds of midges, which dance up and down with delight in the sunshine, and playfully tickle your cheeks with their refined instruments of torture. Without question, these are in a sense drawbacks; but how trifling they are! Most gladly would

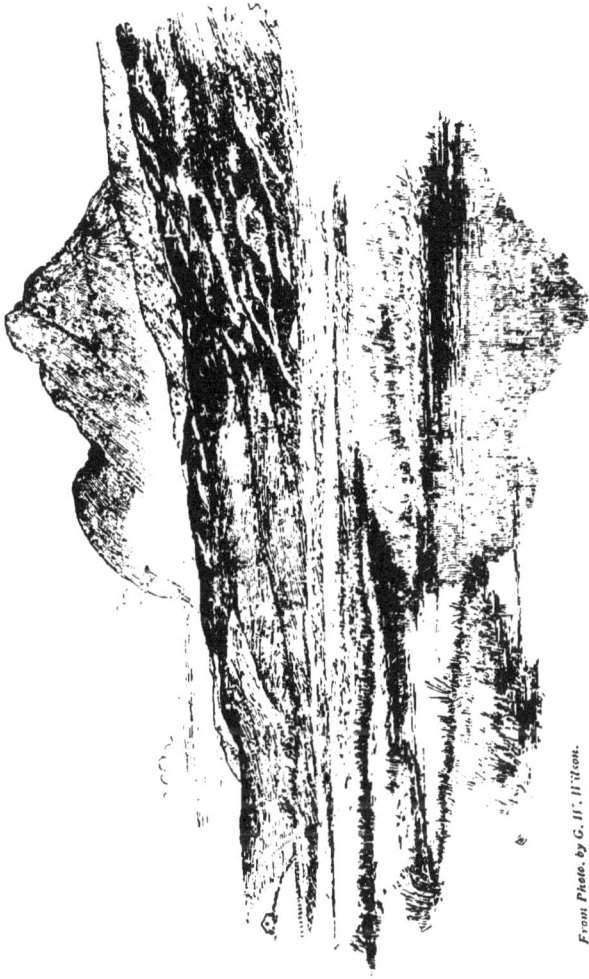

From Photo. by G. W. Wilson.

SUILVEN, ASSYNT, SUTHERLAND.

many of us bear each and all of them in their seasons to
escape the inanities, vulgarities, and arrogancies of the
modern trotting tourist. Moreover, see how much you
gain by walking! You exercise and strengthen your
limbs, absorbing fresh air and health in the manner most
truly natural; you talk with a congenial companion when
and what you please, without noise, interruption, or dis-
cord; you can turn aside when you will to explore a
tempting little glen, or visit the grim ruins of an old
castle; you may lounge for an hour by the way-side to
drink in one of nature's wonderful pictures, or spend a
little well-used time in making some rapid sketches;
and, moreover, you may probe the mind of a passing
native for advice or information—both which are generally as hard to extract as they are worthless when
secured. If these be not attractions sufficient, there are
many more, high and humble alike. You may gather
materials for a great book or lofty-toned lecture; you
can enjoy a cold bath in loch or river or bay; you can
break your journey anywhere or at any time to spend a
day in fishing; and you can stand still to light a cigar
without requiring to employ the hissing fumes of powder
and phosphorus. In short, you are sole and absolute
masters of yourselves, and may with impunity laugh to
scorn the ways of humanity at large.

To any who may contemplate a tour through the
Highlands on foot, I venture to offer two humble remarks. The first is a suggestion—the second a warning.

As we approached the end of our first day's journey,
my friend Ian complained that his feet were very hot

and painful, if not already broken into blisters. Fortunately the latter suspicion turned out to be unfounded ;
and we found a remedy for the existing evil on the
morrow—one known to many, but here recorded for the
benefit of the few. Be sure you carry in your knapsack
a piece of good soap. Meantime I shall not recommend
any in particular, but in view of a second edition I am
open to offers from advertisers, any consideration I may
ask being strictly moderate and reasonable. After starting in the morning, stop at the first burn by the wayside,
take off your boots, plunge your feet—stockings and
all—into the water, then rub them all over with the soap
until the lather is like the foaming must,

> " Round the white feet of laughing girls
> Whose sires have marched to Rome."

When you have pulled on your boots again, do not mind
if the rich creamy froth oozes from the tops—(you bade
the young ladies Good-bye before you left)—you will
walk as on the softest wool for several hours. If by-and-
by the feet become hot again, you may lift some water
with your fingers and drop it into the sides of your boots,
by which process the fermentation will at once be
renewed. After a few days' walking, the feet will require no thought or care whatever. On our second
day's march, Ian adopted this plan, and covered his
thirty-five miles in perfect comfort.

My second remark must assume the form of a warning, and is specially intended for those who are students
of the classics, if they are zealous in the pursuit of learn-

ing. The advice may also be useful to ardent and
generous friends of the parties whom I have just described. What is the use of us in this world if we
cannot give others the benefit of our experience? Here,
of course, I ought to quote "footprints on the sands of
time," &c.; but I am merciful, and refrain. My counsel
is very simple; it is simply this—Don't carry in your
knapsack an Analytical Hebrew Lexicon. Wae's me! I
did it—did it to oblige my friend, who was very shortly
to face a college examination in that ancient tongue.
The idea was that he might study a little in the calm of
the evening, when the fatigues of the day were over, and
that my help and that of the Lexicon might be useful to
him. The experiment was not the success we expected.
My views on the subject have undergone a change.
After that time—in fact, more than a score of years ago
—I made up my mind, upon careful consideration, never
to undertake the same service again for Ian or anybody
else. It may seem severe to say it, but I believe it was
mistaken kindness on the part of Ian to give me the
opportunity of showing that real kindness to him. Many
and many a time did I groan in secret because of, not
the load of my learning, but—which is a very different
thing—my load of learning. On level ground I felt like
a poor hunchback bearing a load I could not see, while,
among big stones and lumpy heather, every jump and
jolt sent inwards through my shoulder blades a strong
sense of my personal virtue and benevolence. At the
same time, I must not be unfair to my friend. His
knapsack was less capacious than mine, and could not

hold the Lexicon. Knowing this, Ian often offered to carry mine for me, but I would not hear of his doing so. The delight of piling up so much daily merit—for a whole fortnight, remember—was too sweet to be lightly thrown or bartered away. Must I here make a confession? Can it be that what I have said about my friend has been written to propitiate him, for he writes in London magazines, and wields a caustic pen? In a few weeks he may be the critic of these pages! Oh Ian! I shall carry the Lexicon again for you; yes, I shall,—if you can find no one else.

Our first day's walk, from Golspie to Ardgay, was our shortest—only some seventeen miles, if I remember aright. From the second stage onward, our average was about twenty-four—a distance which became easier every day. The route we chose from Golspie—shorter far than the present railway line—lay first between level fields in high cultivation, then upward and still upward over a broad mass of mountain and moor, like an elephant's back with its steep, sloping sides. Until Bonar Bridge is reached, there is not much either to attract or interest in the outward features of the country. Therefore I shall take the opportunity of gathering a few jottings from the human side of things.

A friend of mine, whose name without leave asked and granted I would not mention, is my authority for the particulars which follow; and in that respect he has no superior in the northern counties. He had some occasion, many years ago, to examine carefully certain of the old ecclesiastical records of the parish of Creich, which lies at the inner end and on the northern shore of the Dornoch Firth. Among much that was valuable and interesting, he found also some entries which were quaint and amusing enough. These, very curiously, appear to have occurred chiefly in matters of finance. Here are a few specimens—not perhaps intended to serve the purpose to which I venture to put them.

In an old Kirk-Session record, there is reference made on one of the pages, to a "Collection for the Northern Infirmity," but I forget the sum which had been contributed. Prosaic persons of " vinegar aspect," as Shakespeare puts it, might be foolish enough to suggest that the last three letters should be " -ary ;" but such a correction would be to destroy all the suggestiveness of the entry, and put a damper on humour and speculation alike. Pushing it aside, we proceed to investigate the subject seriously. What is, *par excellence*, the Northern Infirmity ? Is it pride, or craft, or greed, or some other unknown and equally pardonable weakness ? Let the conscience of every clansman who reads this page give an answer. How strange too, that a collection should be the remedy ! I have indeed heard of mental affections cured by material means. Many of us remember the question and answer :

> " O dear, doctor, what will cure love !
> The shaking of the hand, and the pulling off the glove ; "

but the case before us is still more remarkable ; for here we have an "infirmity" for which the cure is—not perhaps pounds, but at least shillings and pence. Yet here also we detect a touch of kinship between north and south. Did not a wealthy churchman, many years ago, seeking a cure for some of Scotland's ecclesiastical ailments, ask the question, " Will siller (money) dae't?" Here in Creich we find indications of a similar medicine; let us hope that the remedy was ample and effectual.

The next entry which I shall quote is very mysterious. Perhaps it is too much to hope that, after so long a lapse of time, the true solution will ever be found. It runs as follows : " To 2 men chasing 1 woman for 3 days, 7s. 6d." It is just possible that this may have been an episode in some case of discipline, but every logician knows that "may have been" is no evidence, but rather a treacherous quicksand. We therefore leave the whole case to the wisdom, individual or collective, of those who read this book, but regret that we cannot offer a prize for the best solution of the problem.

The third extract is at first sight the most remarkable of all. Here is a simple and significant money transaction : " To mending the minister's preaching, 1s. 6d." In this case again, a wide vista opens for inquiry. We are left to conjecture as to those respects in which the minister's preaching was defective, or had fallen into disrepair. The extract relates to times when ministers in the Highlands were surely "soond" enough in all conscience, that is to say, before innovations were invented, or Biblical criticism had ventured out of its den. This, however, is not the chief point to be noticed. It matters little, to us at least, what was wrong with the minister's preaching; the great lesson for this generation is to notice how easily and cheaply it was put to rights. Let us suppose an advertisement on the same lines as the account before us : " Preachers cured of their defects and errors—only 1s. 6d. per head." Just imagine what a prospect! The modest sum of £75 would repair the preaching of a thousand ministers, in the Free Kirk or the Auld. But what—what is this? No wonder I feel angry now when a fairy imp on my shoulder hints that the word "tent" should follow "preaching," and that the reference is to the outdoor pulpit used at Communion seasons. Does not orthodoxy compel us to object to this suggestion? We all know what mischiefs and miseries have arisen from words interpolated in ancient documents like these.

Our last quotation from these records is one on which perhaps the least said the better, for the subject is a painful one to all who know the doctrine of human frailty. Here is the entry, but for obvious reasons I suppress the name : " To ---— ——— for additional sinning at the time of the communion." What can be said of such a case? An old woman once said that the doctrine of human depravity was a "blessed doctrine, if we would only live up to it ; " but here we have the difficulty solved in a practical manner which leaves nothing to be desired. It was once suggested to me that the word " sinning " should be " singing ; " but the person who offered such a correction must have been a hot partizan of the offender, or a man ignorant of human nature, or perhaps both these in one.

G

By the Bridge of Bonar, we crossed southward out of Sutherlandshire into Ross-shire, and slept at Ardgay Inn, about a mile from the march between the two counties. Our aim in the first portion of our tour was to cross the northern portion of Ross-shire from the German Ocean to the Atlantic, and then to bend our steps northward along the entire west coast of Sutherland.

The first part of this programme was a stiff piece of work. The distance from Ardgay on the Dornoch Firth to Ullapool on Loch Broom is not less than thirty-five miles. For greater part of the way, we had no road whatever ; and, with the exception of a few houses near to either end, there was not a spot where we could rest for the night.

Having duly observed the precept which promises to make one " healthy, wealthy, and wise," we left Ardgay on a fine fresh morning early in July. Behind us, and beyond the winding reaches of the Dornoch Firth, the sun had risen from his bed far out in the German Ocean, and was spreading his warm brilliance lower and lower down upon the hillsides. He always paints from the sky downwards in the morning, and from the sea-level upwards in the evening. With joy we welcomed his growing light ; and we hoped by-and-by, our journey ended, to see him draw his evening curtains about him over the Atlantic waves. For some miles we passed through a fertile strath, and then bending to the right, left the Kirk and Manse of Croick behind us, and sallied forth upon a wild wilderness of mountain and valley, beyond which—somewhere on this side of Canada—lay our destination for the night. What a day of stern and hard-won enjoyment we had! In among piles of mountains we wended our way—here jauntily tripping down a narrow glen, there scrambling upon hands and feet over a projecting shoulder—at one time slipping and stumbling among the sliding debris of a *scree*, at another pitching and plunging among knee-deep banks of heather. For miles and miles not a trace of humankind was to be seen —not even a road to point the way on, or back, to human society. How cheerfully did we dispense among wilds so glorious, and under a sun so brilliant, with man and commerce and art and all their petty belongings! Nature, sternly beautiful, charmingly grand, wrapped us round body and soul in her sweet fellowship. Even life, save in the soft mosses and shaggy heather, seemed strangely absent. White masses of mist, as the sun mounted high, rose from their couches in the bays of the mountains, and fleecy fragments,

> " Hanging so light, and hanging so high,
> On the topmost ridge that looks up at the sky,"

mounted up and hovered for a while over the spot where they had rested. These seemed for a time to have life and breath, but the growing sunshine melted them into the strong blue of noontide, and ere long they were gone. Nothing that appeared to live remained, save the coveys of grouse which rose at times on our approach and fluttered frantically away over the heather, or the drowsy wild-bee straggling here and there among the purple tufts. Most of all were we attracted and entranced by the majestic and ever-changing forms of the mountains. At every ascent and descent, at every bend to right and left, at every minute's advance, changes grew before our eyes. Conical peaks became ridges, while ridges again mounted into cones ; smooth shoulders dropped into frowning scars, and rounded summits became cleft into mitres ; groups of mountain-tops scattered themselves into chains ; and slopes which seemed to meet and cross each other opened suddenly to disclose some sweet valley between. Every hillside and hollow had its rivulet or stream, each one bubbling or murmuring to its listening banks—all hustling onward and downward to their un-known destinies on the far-off coasts, while here and there the flickering face of a loch hid their waters from view for a while, as they rested from their rush and song.

Right in the heart of the mountains, not long after mid-day, we had quite a little adventure. We arrived at a stage in our journey where we did not know in what direction to steer, whether straight forward over the sloping spur of a hill, or down toward the left into a broad green valley. We chose the latter course—chiefly I daresay because it looked like a glen in which we might find a human dwelling and ask for guidance. Perhaps we were also attracted by the sight of the majestic Ben Dearag—the red mountain—whose head, more than 3500 feet high, and the weighty epaulets on his shoulders closed up the glen toward the south. At length we came in sight of a cottage and outhouses nestling under a hillside, with varied patches of cultivated ground in front. No human beings were visible, except two young girls who were busily hoeing turnips in a field, and to them we resolved to make an appeal. We soon found that they knew no English, and the discovery was embarrassing to both parties. However, they laughed and we laughed; and all four were the better of the outburst. Then I summoned up courage to try my Gaelic, and asked the way to Ullapool, in reply to which we received most copious directions. One of the girls pointed north, and then west, and then south, described curves with her hand in the air, directed her finger first to one side and then to the other of a long lofty hill, and all the while poured forth an eloquent torrent of Gaelic beneath which my scanty knowledge of the language was hopelessly submerged. As the best thing to do in the circumstances, we had another hearty and unanimous round of laughter.

By this time an old man had appeared at the cottage door, and was watching us with evident curiosity and interest. He seemed to be asking himself "for what strange cause" Ian and I had

> "Sought those wilds traversed by few,
> Without a pass from Roderick Dhu,"

or some other authority. My friend suggested that we should try him; but I argued that, if the younger generation knew no English, it was hopeless to expect such an attainment in a man far advanced in years. Still, we resolved to make the experiment, for we were desperate. If we found no one to set us on the right route again, it was impossible to say where we might be

landed, or what might happen, if we were overtaken by
darkness. So we approached the cottage and, greeting
the old man, I asked him,

"Have you any English ? "

The corners of his mouth rose perceptibly ; his eyes
twinkled slily between their half-closed lashes, and he
startled us with the reply,

"Hoots, maun, 'a hae nae Gaulic !"

Of course we were delighted, and soon found ourselves on the best of terms with the old man. We told
him of the difficulty we had with the girls, and we had
his fullest sympathy. In fact, it is well for his good
name that I cannot now recall the highly spiced language
he used regarding them because of ignorance for which,
poor lassies ! they were not to blame. Our friend was a
shepherd from the Scotch side of the Cheviot Hills, and
he soon told us his story. Thirty years before, a wealthy
sheep farmer had induced him to come north and tend
the flocks over a wide "run" in these wilds ; but it was
very evident that he had not been, and never would be,
naturalized in central Ross. It grieves me to tell that
he was as blind as a mole to the glories of the mountain
scenery around him, and that he frankly avowed his
determination never to defile his lips with a single word
of "their abominable Gaulic." Even his young dogs,
though Highlanders by birth, were named after the
"Tyne" and the "Tweed." We enjoyed a long crack
with the shepherd, and before we parted he gave us sufficient directions for the way. The truth was, we should
not have come down that glen at all ; but we were pleased

rather than otherwise with the little episode into which our blunder had led us.

For about ten miles from the shepherd's cottage onwards, the route was fearfully rough, and not a little toilsome. Again and again we were glad to sit down and rest our limbs on some flat stone and smoke a pipe the while. The Lexicon did not help or console me in the smallest degree, nor did his high culture do anything for my friend. Only bone and muscle were of any value. To these trackless, weary, rugged miles, one might almost apply the words of the Australian poet,

" Education and English polish are very unsaleable stuff,
   The men we want in Melbourne must be sent out here in the rough."

Happily, whether like men " in the rough " or in a polished state, we reached at last a " made " road, and found ourselves only eight miles from Ullapool. It was now near six o'clock, and we span along merrily to our destination in less than two hours. The sun had made better speed than we had done, for when we came in sight of the sea, he was travelling far down the western sky, but still looking out upon us from between purple folds of cloud above and ragged golden banks below. Before seeking the hospitality of friends, we washed our faces and hands, first in the briny Atlantic, and then in a noisy streamlet, which would perhaps not have been so merry if it had known that it was rushing on to near burial in the ocean. How soundly we slept that night, serenaded by soft murmurs from the Atlantic surges! Not less cheerfully did we rise with the lark next morning to resume our journey.

The western shores of Sutherlandshire are deeply indented, extremely tortuous in their windings, and peculiarly rugged in contour.   They form a base-line to scenery wilder and grander than anywhere else in Scotland, except among the Cuchullin hills in Skye.   So much may be said of that entire seaboard from the borders of Ross-shire on the south to the storm-lashed cliffs of Cape Wrath on the north.   But the *ne plus ultra* of that scenery lies in a wide circuit round Loch Assynt, which we reached from Ullapool after a walk of twenty-four miles.   Take a stroll from the hotel at Inchnadamph a few miles to the southward, and when you turn your face toward the setting sun, what a panorama do you behold!

Away to the south-west there rise sheer up from the long sweeping undulations of a great plateau the pyramidal peaks of Coulmore and Coulbeg—twin sisters which rear their storm-beaten heads more than 2500 feet in air.   Between and behind them lies a third mountain-top, Stack Polly, somewhat lower and quainter in form than the other two.   In bird's eye view, they must form a triangle whose three sides are exactly equal in length. Now turn and look straight to the westward.   Lo! there are two lofty cone-like mountains, not yet worn down into pyramids.   The more westerly is Suilven, 2400 feet high, its summit carved into a deep saddle-back; the other to the east is Canisp, or Canisb, nearly 2800 feet high, the loftiest of all the five.   Now, all these mountains are not simply of similar, but of the same formation, and they have their wonderful history more or less legibly scribbled on their checks.   Suffer me to tell it in a few

brief sentences ; it is well worth turning aside to tell
and to hear.

The under-lying formation on which all this district
rests is gneiss, which spreads out, like the sea after a
storm, in long, low waves, with damp, mossy hollows and
shallow tarns between. Over this flat-lying gneiss there
is built up layer upon layer of Old Red Sandstone of the
Cambrian system, not less than four or five thousand
feet thick. In process of time, long, long ages gone by,
this solid table-land of sandstone has been ploughed up
and washed away, no one knows whither, by glacial
currents, but the mountain masses which I have named
refused to yield, and have stood their ground ever since.
These sturdy giants have seen all the thick beds of rock
swept clean away from between them, yet have themselves survived the icy floods. You can see on their
sides the layers of Cambrian rock like tiers of masonry :
and if you run your eye from one to another, and
from that to another again, you can observe that
the lines on each are on a level with those of its
neighbours, because once upon a time they were parts
of one continuous bed. The process in all probability
occupied much the same number of years as the slow and
patient detrition of the Black Rock chasm, so that if you
feel yourself competent to name a figure in the one case,
you may venture to do the same in the other as well.
These stately cones and pyramids, with their frosted
heads, lie like a cluster of beads to the south of Loch
Assynt, but they do not exhaust the mountain glories of
the district. To the east and north of the loch, lofty and

imposing heights crowd in upon its shores. Of these, three mighty monarchs of rock command the attention of the traveller, and demand special notice.

Enthroned above the eastern end of the loch sits the double-headed Ben More, 3200 feet high, like Saul among the people as compared even with the giants around him. Further to the north rises the grim Glasven, 2500 feet high, with tiny lochs nestling close under its beetling sides. To the west again, over against these two, lies the huge, shapeless mass of Quinaig, in many respects the most wonderful of them all. If it were possible to look down upon Quinaig, as the eagle does, from the upper sky, we should see her three summits beneath us like the famous triple symbol of the Isle of Man. The highest spur is 2600 feet high ; the other two are very little lower and viewed from beneath look not less lofty. The mountain, like another Janus, presents one face to Loch Assynt, lying at its feet in the sunshine, another to Lochs Cairnbawn and Glencoul, which crouch low beneath its northern and eastern shadows. Ben Quinaig is of the same formation as the five heights which run southward to meet the Ross-shire mountains, but she differs from them in that she wears a white cap of quartz, which sparkles bravely in the sunlight.

Amid this galaxy of great peaks, often wreathed in whirling vapour, lies Loch Assynt, like a long leaf tapering at either end, its waters rich in the noble trout, and its shores fringed with the graceful mountain-loving birch. Near its eastern end stand the picturesque ruins of Ardvreck, or Advrock, Castle, the " bannered home "

for many a day of the brave Macleods, and in later years
a stronghold of the Mackenzies. Many a fight and feud
have these now lonely walls seen ; many a romance lies
buried in the story they refuse to tell. But I shall
return presently to these old haunts of chivalry and
cruelty.

On our arrival at the homely hotel of Inchnadamph, we
had abundant food, first for the wants of the outer
man, then for the higher exercises of reflection and con-
verse. Our minds and hearts were filled with the
inspiration of the gorgeous scenery around us. No
wonder, therefore, that I must add a word of confession. This was the second evening on which the
precious Lexicon was allowed undisturbed repose. Ian
did not seem at all guilty or ashamed when, at bed-
time, I mischievously showed him a small corner
peeping out of my knapsack.

During a stroll after our hearty evening repast, we
took the road which skirts the northern shore of Loch
Assynt. The fast-declining sun was throwing slanting
bands of gorgeous light down upon the glistening waters.
We reached by-and-by the ruins of Edderachalda, huge,
ungainly, roofless, with double gables and a hideous
chimney stalk. The Mackenzies built it for a residence
nearly two centuries ago, but it was destroyed by fire
some fifty years later. No one knows who the incendiary
was, but he almost deserves a monument to his memory.
The only pity is that, when he set about the destruction
of the ungainly mass, he was not able to sweep its very
remains out of sight. No wonder that Quinaig every

day frowns down upon them in his anger. By way of contrast, how attractive are the stately ruins of Ardvrock, looking us straight in the face as we cross the narrow neck of the peninsula on which they stand! It was without doubt the scene of

"Many a wassail wild and deed of blood;"

but now there is not a cat to mew, nor a cock to crow, in the fortress of the Clan Macleod. The castle was originally three storeys high, and was surmounted by a lofty circular tower. In 1650, the famous Marquis of Montrose was taken prisoner by Neil Macleod, the Chief of Assynt, and imprisoned within these walls. He had been signally defeated at Fearn, in the east of Ross-shire, and so his singular career of victory came to an end. Accompanied by a young officer named Sinclair, Montrose fled into the mountainous wilds of Sutherland, and there suffered many privations. It is even said that at one time his hunger was so great that he was fain to eat his gloves. After a short confinement in Ardvrock, Macleod surrendered his prisoner to the authorities, who had offered a handsome reward for his capture. The only recompense which the Chief of Assynt received was forty bolls of oatmeal. Surely the prize was worth a richer reward.

Dark and wild as are the ruins of Ardvrock, there is a singular subtle charm in their loneliness. Do not the wasting walls and crumbling corners seem to say, "We have no part or lot in this age; let us alone to sink down and die; then perhaps Mother Earth will cover our graves with grassy sod? We cannot tell our secrets;

they are not for modern ears. The clan is broken ; the chiefs and bards are gone ; the days of romance and glory are past, and we are fain to follow." Somehow we love even the evidences of age on these blighted battlements ; the very wounds and scars inflicted by the hand of time delight both the eye and the heart. On the evening of our visit, every aspect of nature invited us to linger and enjoy. To the west rose the fast-purpling hills between us and the sea ; at our feet lay the calm loch, with a heaven on its face looking up to its birthplace above ; northward, the nearer faces of Quinaig mounted upward to the heavens—the sun painting rainbows of colour on their scars ; behind us, the steep sides of a narrow, craggy glen sloped upward to the ponderous swelling mass of Ben More standing aloof as in proud disdain from the society of meaner mountains and of men.

We returned to our hotel through multitudinous mists of midges ; and were thankful to escape within doors. On the road in front, two gallant pipers strode to and fro, discoursing sweet music, and evidently proud of their gifts. We thought it might be said of them in flexible French, as some one said of someone else, that they played *fort bien* and at the same time *bien fort*. We had material enough for many a fantastic dream in the sights and sounds, the fights and fairies, the men and midges, of which our waking hours had been full. If in Assynt anyone is troubled with night-mare, the thought of these mighty mountain-masses creeping over him and crushing him down to the earth's centre would surely make his misery tolerably, or if you like, intolerably, complete. Some such idea as this once moved the fond pupil of a geologist to poetry. He greatly loved and admired his teacher, and thus expressed his devotion :

"Where *shall* we our great Professor inter,
   That in peace may rest his bones ?
If we hew him a rocky sepulchre,
   He'll rise and break the stones,
And examine each stratum that lies around,
For he's quite in his element underground."

The Gaelic word "Assynt" is a compound, and signifies "out and in." If so, like almost all place-names in the Highlands, it is most fitting and felicitous. Indeed it applies admirably, not only to the district so called, but to the entire west coast of Sutherland from the borders of Ross-shire to Cape Wrath itself. Looking for instance at the map, we can still see in the endless contortions of the shore, as we used to do when children, the figures and profiles of men and beasts—not one of them in any degree like to any other. There are brows flat and high on the headlands ; eyes large and small in the lochs and tarns ; noses Roman, Grecian, retroussè, on the rocky capes ; bay-mouths wide and narrow, open and shut, drooping in sadness, curving upward in joy ; chins which are impudent, and chins which are retiring ; cheeks smooth and furrowed, shaven and bearded ; and in all these you can clearly see, if you have any discernment at all, grumpy grandfathers and grinning fools, laughing children and scolding dominies, gaping crocodiles and snarling monkeys, weeping maids and wistful lovers. The surface of the country inland from the shore is extremely varied, rugged, and wild, but full of interest

and charm for healthy and buoyant natures. If you believe, as I for one do, that in order to see the beauties and
taste the sweets of land and water and sky there is needed
not only sight but *insight*, which is something far more
and better, you will find at every turn of the highway
new matter of surprise and admiration. Island-studded
bays like Badcall ; picturesque retreats like Scourie ;
deeply-indented lochs like Laxford—the " Fiord of sal-
mon ;" distant views of a mountain-chain of peaks ;
long successions of rocky knolls crowned with brushwood
and heather : these are a few of the elements which go
to make up the panorama between Assynt and the Kyle
of Durness. When at length you look down over
the brindled cliffs of Cape Wrath ; when you behold
its rugged masses of God-made masonry ; when you hear
the thunder-throb of the waves in its vaulted caverns ;
when you gaze to south and west and north over
the hungry heaving sea ; you can but look and
marvel and adore. You are indeed made of inferior
mettle if you do not find your surprise grow into an
inspiring wonder and your admiration into a solemn
ecstasy.

More than fifty years ago, there lived in the neighbourhood of this stern, stormy headland one who because of
her robust Christian character was called " the woman of
the great faith." Perhaps the religious element in her
nature was, like the beautiful seaweed,

" Nursed by the ocean and rocked by the storms."

On one occasion, when travelling southward on the top

of a stage-coach, she entered into friendly conversation with a gentleman, who soon discovered that his companion was no ordinary woman. At length he took the liberty of asking whence she had come and whither she was going. Choosing for the nonce to answer in a spiritual and allegorical sense, she gave the beautiful reply, " I have come from Cape Wrath, and I am going to the Cape of Good Hope."

During our journey from Cape Wrath along the north coast toward Caithness, my friend Ian and I spent one memorable night under the roof of a well-to-do and hospitable farmer. It grieves me to say that his extensive sheep ground was once dotted over with the loved homes of many families, long since burnt out, or driven out, or perhaps both, from their native straths and hillsides. These things were done in the dark eviction days of Sutherland. Even the natural tokens of their presence there at one period have been carefully and purposely swept out of sight. Only here and there a few stones or groups of grassy ridges indicate where crofter dwellings once stood. An old woman, who had so been driven from hearth and home, once revisited the scenes of her early and happy life. On her return from Sutherland again, she was asked by some old neighbours what she had seen. Filled with grief and fired with indignation, her reply was very significant, " I saw the raven's nest in your old home, and dogs kennelled in the minister's study." Happily, in Sutherland at least, these days are long gone by—never, I trust, to return again. That policy of eviction was little in accordance with worldly wisdom—not to say justice or humanity.

When Ian and I approached the commodious farm-house, we suspected at once that something unusual was going on. When the front door was opened, we could at once see and hear that the house was full of company. On making this discovery, our immediate impulse was to leave our cards and proceed upon our way. We had an inn four miles behind us to which we might return, and another only thirty miles before us (it was now sunset) to which we might push forward. However, we were not allowed to do either the one or the other. On being informed by the servant, the farmer himself at once appeared and insisted that we should join the company and stay over night. Some shift or other would be made to provide us with sleeping room.

Well, stay the night we did, and it *was* a night! The company numbered from twenty to thirty, and a kindlier, happier, merrier thirty—not to speak of winsomeness, beauty, and the like—I had never met before and have never met since. Music, dancing, supper, and parlour pastimes stole away the hours unawares and it was early morning before anyone thought of retiring. At length we wished each other a good sleep all round—oh! what irony on the part of certain persons—and departed to our several chambers.

Ian and I occupied a small bedroom together, while two young gentlemen from Caithness shared the next adjoining. We could hear each other's voices through the wall. All of us were brimming over with excitement.

H

When my friend and I had closed the door, we sat down to calm ourselves and discuss the events of the evening. Possibly the ladies also came in for a share of comment, but that I do not distinctly remember. All at once— probably about 2 A.M.—we were startled by a wild, pro- longed howl of pain from the next room. How loud and shrill ! methinks I can hear it even now ! It must have pierced every chamber and corner even of that com- modious house. Most probably it awoke all the sheep dogs outside and set them a howling also in sympathy or defiance, for such is their wont in such a crisis. What could it mean ? Burglary, murder, suicide, sudden insanity, toothache, assault and battery, which was it, or what ? We sprang together to our door only to find— that we could not open it. Had an earthquake twisted the side-posts or lintel ? We shouted to ask what was the matter, but heard no voice in reply—only a faint, far- off ripple of sound like the giggling of mermaids sporting in the loch. At length our friends shouted through the wall that they, too, were helpless ; they could not open their door. Ere long, however, we discovered the reason. Wicked hands—how true it is that there is much human nature in us all !—had fastened the handles of the two doors together with rope ; and therefore it was no wonder that for a time we tugged and pulled in vain. At length we were victorious ; we forced our door open a little, a knife did the rest, and we rushed into our friends' room, ready for ambulance work or any other form of aid which might be needed. Then, in a few hasty, breathless words, we heard from the lips of the sufferer himself the whole sad story. It was simply this. Before we retired, some of the young ladies had visited our rooms, had folded down the sheets, and had strewed our beds with sharp prickly whins, chopped up small and delicately sprinkled all over. After we had said good night, one of the young gentlemen next door, rapidly undressing and having almost reached a nude condition, had thrown back the upper coverings and sprung in with a leap and bound—to his pain and sorrow and shame. Despairing and forbearing, I shall not attempt to describe either his condition or his feelings; happily for me, I did not share in either, except by way of weeping sympathy. Any readers who are themselves devoid of all imagination must just be content and pass on.

Nor need I linger in detail over the sequel of my story. Springing, each one of us, into a fair proportion of our clothing, we sallied out most valiantly into the lobbies and staircases. There all the rest of the company were already gathered, and were discussing, in groups here and there, the sad fate of the young man. As the same doom was benevolently intended for us, Ian and I joined the party of revenge. Our weapons were towels well soaked in the ewers of water, and with these we laid about us vigorously; but I shall not go into further detail. Very soon the lobbies were empty and dark, and we retired from the field of battle. Before dawn the house had sunk into stillness; and that same morning, long ere the sun peeped over the hills to see if we were coming, we were off and away on our tramp toward Caithness.

Perhaps it was well for us, on the night of the adventure just recorded, that an excellent minister, who once lived in this quarter of the world, was no longer in the body. He might perchance have heard of our doings, and come in upon us in the midst of our revelry. I can conceive of no excuse we could have given, unless we followed the example of our first father Adam, and laid the blame on the other sex. No one could deny that the ladies had of their own accord provoked the engagement. Well, this worthy old man was a sworn enemy to dancing. In this intense antipathy he had perhaps some reason after all, for in his day and parish the practice really seems to have become an abuse. The natives, especially the young people, met frequently, sometimes almost every night, in each other's houses, and danced until morning dawned. This custom prevailed even when there was no special occasion, such as a marriage or a ball, for the revelry.

One night the minister heard some sounds about the house, and, on going to find out what they were, discovered that some one had assisted his two servant girls out of a garret window, and that they were off, without leave asked or obtained, to the dancing. What was to be done? It vexed the old minister sorely to think that some even of his own household should be act and part in such scenes. Fortunately, that important functionary the beadle, or church-officer, always in his own esteem the second—or including the laird the third—man in the parish, was within easy reach. Probably he was also minister's man, and lived above the stable or in

a cottage near by. To him his master fully confided the
story of his grief. In the same breath he ordered George,
for that was the beadle's name, to proceed at once to the
scene of wild gaiety and bring the lasses home without
fail and without delay. The faithful servant started on
his midnight errand with the very best intentions as to
doing his master's behests, but, alas! for the frailty of
human nature, even in a beadle! When George entered
the festive gathering to seek the wandering sheep, he
probably thought it would be no great sin to tarry a little
and see the fun. As often happens in such cases, this
delay was his undoing. The stirring notes of the fiddle
or bagpipe were more than he could resist. The old Adam
awoke within him, and what was the result? Flinging
off his coat he plunged into the giddy whirl, and soon
forgot manse, minister, errand, and—what was worst of
all—his own high office, in the frantic wildness of his
enjoyment.

Meantime the minister, waiting and longing for the
return of George and the erring ones, at last grew impatient at the delay, and perhaps even suspicious as to
its cause. Thus it came to pass that, unable to bear the
suspense any longer, he himself issued forth into the
night, and, under a strong sense of duty, found his way
to the scene of action. Here I regret to say that
authentic details are wanting, but a little sober imagination will not lead us far wrong. Now, now, my gentle
reader, don't you begin to picture the good old minister
casting aside his upper garment like the beadle, and
himself tripping the "light fantastic toe." No such

thing ; he was double proof against so worldly a temptation ; and I cannot betray his good name even to make
the story more symmetrically complete.   No, no ; when
he entered there must have been an abrupt hush, a
sudden paralysis of flying feet, an utter breakdown of
laughter and joke.   Would not the fiddle subside with a
squeak, or the pipes die out in a wail ?   Even the wild
orgies of Alloway Kirk did not more suddenly cease,
when Tam o' Shanter commended the exertions of Cutty
Sark.

Finally, when the revellers were scattered, we can
picture the funeral-like procession home—the minister
stalking on in front, sad indeed, but so far satisfied—
the beadle and maids, silent and cowed, but probably
not less wicked in heart than before.

My friend and I tramped on our wandering way along
the north coast of Sutherland, and at length entered the
county of Caithness.   After a brief stay in Thurso, we
paid a visit—neither the first nor last for either of us—
to John o' Groat's, the Land's End of the mainland of
Scotland.   Thence we walked to the busy port of Wick,
where we bade each other farewell, though only for a
time.   Memory contains many more scenes and incidents
of our happy walking tour, but these must, for the
present at least, be held *in retentis.*

> " Long, long be my heart with such memories filled !
> Like the vase in which roses have once been distilled :
> You may break, you may ruin the vase if you will,
> But the scent of the roses will hang round it still."

From Photo. by G. H. Wilson.

CASTLES SINCLAIR AND GIRNIGOE.

CHAPTER V.

THIS is intended to be a chapter of mosaics, for it contains many and parti-coloured fragments, pieced together as skilfully as I can, relating to the scenery, people, and traditions of my native county. The above heading has been chosen because the dominant outward feature of interest in Caithness is the almost continuous succession of lofty mural precipices which form the coast line, and because the chief human associations, past and present, of the county, lie along the rugged, rocky fringe of its shores.

This most northern county on the mainland of Scotland has many peculiar, if not unique, features. Occupying the north-east corner of the country, its form is rudely triangular, though the lines are warped and curved by many a cape and bay. The northern side faces the cold Arctic Ocean and the Orkney Islands ; the eastern lies fully open to the wild storms of the North Sea ; while the south-western border, touching these two at their landward extremities and so completing the triangle, runs along the waving line over moor and mountain, which divides the county from Sutherland. On that boundary march there are elevated ridges toward the north, and toward the south clusters of mountains, some of which rise like cones or pyramids over the low moorlands around. Apart from this more elevated strip along the borders of Sutherland, the county of Caithness is for the most part a widely-extended plateau, high above sea level, and varied over most of its surface by shallow valleys and gentle undulations. The dreary and almost treeless character of the interior, with its " moors and mosses many o'," has perhaps no attractions for the ordinary traveller ; and only certain parties, who have themselves come from beyond the " herring-pond," will agree with the American who said that Caithness was "the finest clearance " he had ever seen. Yet there are many who ought to take an interest even in the inland regions of the county. To the geologist, for example, the Old Red Sandstone yields a plentiful crop of fossil remains and other objects well worthy of his attention and study. To the noble Hugh Miller, Caithness was a happy hunting ground from which he gathered rich scientific spoils. Many remember the humorous squib which was suggested by his rambles over the Old Red Sandstone,

> " Tobacco and whisky cost siller,
>   An' meal is but scanty at hame ;
>   But gang to the stane-mason Miller,
>   He'll pang wi' ichth'olites yer wame ;
>   Wi' fish as Agassiz has ca'd them
>   In Greek like themsel's *hard* and *odd*,
>   That were baked in stane pies afore Adam
>   Gie'd names to the haddocks an' cod."

To the antiquarian and historian also, every parish in

the county offers a wide and rich field for research. The cliffs and bays of the coast line are thickly studded with ancient towers and castles. Their battlements and walls exhibit every stage of ruin and decay, but the very winds which whisper and wail around them are scented with romance. To an observant and curious eye, even the tamest valley or barest ridge has something to show. Let any one look at a full-sized Ordnance Survey map of Caithness, and he will find it dotted all over, north, south, east, and west, with the significant words in German lettering, " Picts' Ho." or " Picts' Houses." These were the rude dwellings of the original inhabitants of the county. In many cases the stones have been ruthlessly scattered, and the sites torn up with the plough, yet not a few still remain in a wonderful state of preservation. Some of these houses have been carefully uncovered and examined, and have disclosed objects of interest and value which are fitted to throw much useful light upon the old-world life of the inmates.

These are outward and visible features, but I cannot overlook one which is as real and significant as any of them, though it makes no appeal to the eye of the traveller. We have all seen old maps, on which the real or reputed sites of battles are marked with tiny cross-swords. If the same system were adopted in the drafting of a map of Caithness, the significant signs of old conflicts would be almost as numerous as Picts' houses on the face of the county. No wonder it might be so, for there is an ancient couplet, often quoted to this day, which declares,

"Sinclair, Sutherland, Keith, and Clan Gun,
There never was peace where these four were in."

Here I must make bold to repeat a question to which I
have never yet found or been offered an answer. Why
were the far-famed Mackays omitted from these lines?
Certain I am that they did more fighting in Caithness
than any other clan except their traditional enemies, the
native Sinclairs. Perhaps the gifted poet could not
squeeze an additional name into his line. On the other
hand the Guns, or Gunns, were not particularly prominent in the strifes of these bloody days—at least not in
Caithness—and their omission from the couplet would
do little wrong to history. That being so, I venture to
suggest that in future the couplet should run thus :—

"Sinclair, Sutherland, Keith, and Mackay,
There never was peace when these four were nigh."

If you search the old clan records, you will find yourself
perfectly bewildered with the never-ending, ever-stirring
tale of raid and rapine, duel and skirmish, pitched battle
and chronic warfare, of which these moors and valleys
were the arena for generation after generation. Thus has it
come to pass that it cannot safely be said of almost any
twenty square yards in the county, Here at least no
foeman's blood ever stained the soil. In imagination, yet
with almost no risk of error anywhere, you may sprinkle
the map all over with the fatal sign of the cross-swords.

There can be no question that the coast scenery is the
dominant feature of interest to the traveller in Caithness.
The petty tourist, who pays a flying visit to Wick and

Thurso and then declares he has seen Caithness,
should be banished south of the Grampians at once—to
the Isle of Dogs if you like. Meantime he may skip the
rest of this paragraph, and of several which follow. The
northern shores from Drumholistan in the Reay country
to Duncansbay Head, and the eastern shores from Duncansbay Head to the Ord, are overshadowed throughout
five-sixths of their length, by mile upon mile, mile upon
mile, of brown cliffs, whose brows are firmly knit against
wind and storm, and relax not even in the sunshine.
These rocky flagstone walls have been built up in
hundreds upon hundreds of layers—some of considerable
thickness, like tiers of actual masonry—others thin and
ragged like the uncut leaves of a book lying upon the
table. As an eminent authority has graphically said,
" The faces of the precipices are constantly etched out
in alternate lines of cornice and frieze, on some of which
vegetation finds a footing, while others are crowded with
sea-fowl." This iron-bound coast is withal characterized by
profuse diversity of detail. At close but irregular intervals, the cliffs are cut from top to bottom by deep narrow
ravines called "goes" (pronounced gyoes, in one syllable),
whose walls resound with the breaking of the surf which
heaves between them. Many and marvellous also are the
caves which open their ungainly mouths to the tide and
blast—some narrow and dark like the dens of wild beasts,
others with temple-like interiors of pillar and aisle and
groined roof. Yet again we note another feature of these
iron defences against the ocean. Detached from cliff or
shore stand isolated masses of rock, called " stacks "—

some of equal thickness from base to summit, like broken columns in the forum of Pompeii, others like elongated cones which taper upward and point to the sky above. Without doubt they once formed part of the sea-walls themselves, but storm and wave have cut them off from their parent strata. Disinherited and lonely though they be, they still stand erect and defiant in presence of the attacking foe.

In addition to many smaller indentations of the sea, there are two wide breaks in the rock-walls which are the fence and defence of the county. These are Sinclair Bay on the east coast and the double bay of Thurso and Dunnet on the north. With precipitous cliffs at their seaward extremities, they are fringed with wide sunlit sweeps of yellow sand, where with arched neck and curling mane may be seen

> "The white steeds of ocean that leap
> With a hollow and wearisome roar."

No one needs to be told, and yet no one can fully realise, how dangerous and deadly this coast has ever been to the "toilers of the deep," sailors and fishermen alike. Many a brave life has been quenched, and many a stout craft dashed into fragments off these cruel heights. Over these things it is no shame to drop a tear ; but not to all, nor at all times, have they been occasion of grief. We are taught to pray "for those in peril on the sea," but I fear this was not always the spirit of those who dwelt on the Caithness seaboard. To many, even in days not very long gone by, a wreck on the coast was a godsend—a

kind providence, for the chance of plunder was too good
to be foolishly despised or thrown away. We need not
wonder that this should be the opinion of any or every
man who was a self-elected and self-appointed "receiver
of wreck!" There were in the good old days many such
native officials, and ofttimes they even quarrelled over
their individual rights and privileges.

As there were not a few of this way of thinking in the
far north, it will surprise no one to learn that the erection of lighthouses on our headlands and skerries was not
regarded with much favour. Many were not much concerned even to hide or disguise their disapproval. One
of these, a grim, northern fisherman, expressed his mind
slily but plainly enough to Mr Stevenson, the noted
lighthouse engineer. The latter had on one occasion
hired a boat to carry him somewhere on an errand of
duty. As they sped along, Mr Stevenson, in a tone of
interest and sympathy, said to the boatman,

"How is it that your sails are so poor and tattered?"

The skipper was equal to the occasion, for he replied
with some emphasis,

"If it hed been God's wull that ye hedna built
sae mony lichthooses, I wud hae gotten new sails last
winter."

It is not likely that Mr Stevenson pursued that line of
conversation further; the boatman was evidently not one
who was very open to conviction on the subject. Besides, all questions which lie on the border line between
divine sovereignty and human responsibility are full of
risk and difficulty. It would be wise on the whole to

avoid controversy regarding them. One of our modern poets goes so far as to suggest that the sea itself considers it very good sport to hurl vessels on their doom and force the hot tears of many a wife and mother. Does not Swinburne speak of

> " the noise of seaward storm that mocks
> With roaring laughter from reverberate rocks
> The cry of ships near shipwreck " ?

If the scenery of Caithness is in many respects unique, so are the people, by which I mean the great majority of the inhabitants. As to race and blood, they stand out in bold relief from the natives of any other part of Great Britain, but are closely allied to the islanders of Orkney and Shetland. You remember how Daniel Defoe treats this subject in his famous cynical piece, "The True-born Englishman," a defence of William of Orange against the race prejudices of his day. After enumerating the various elements, Romans, Gauls, Saxons, Danes, Picts, and others, out of which the English nation has been formed, he goes on to say,

> " From this amphibious, ill-born mob began
> That vain, ill-natured thing, an Englishman.
> The customs, sirnames, languages, and manners
> Of all these nations are their own explainers :
> Whose relics are so lasting and so strong,
> They've left a shibboleth upon our tongue ;
> By which with easy search you may distinguish
> Your Roman-Saxon-Danish-Norman-English."

The poet had good reason to scourge such a mongrel people for their pretended or boasted purity of blood ; but to the people of Caithness the reproach of mixed elements scarcely at all applies. As briefly as possible let me try to tell their story.

Who may have inhabited Caithness or any other part of our islands in the days of Moses no one can tell, and no one is the worse for his ignorance. We must come down nearly to the beginning of the Christian era before we get into our fingers any threads of fact regarding the early occupation of Britain. One or two centuries before Christ, powerful tribes of Aryan origin spread over Western Europe, and crossed over also to the British Isles. Some say they came from Central Asia, some say from the northern slopes of the Alps, some say from the southern shores of the Baltic, some say from Africa and Spain; as to the actual whence, there is no real certainty. They were, however, the Celtic branch of the Aryan family, and after their settlement in Britain, were driven westward and northward by the Jutes, Saxons, and Angles, who came after them from the Continent at a later period.

One branch of the Celts retreated into Wales and Cornwall, another possessed themselves of Ireland, the Isle of Man, and the Scottish Highlands, even as far north as Caithness. As for the old aborigines, few and weak as they probably were, they must have been either extinguished or absorbed by the invaders, who for all practical purposes may be considered the primitive inhabitants of the country, at least in historic times. Thus the Celtic hordes—to whom probably the name Picts or Picti first belonged, because some of them painted their persons—occupied Caithness for some time before, and for several centuries after, the birth of Christ. Then came a great, though a gradual revolution, the beginning of which dates from the year 780 or thereabouts. The Norse and Danish Vikings—so named from their sheltering and skulking in the "viks" or bays—began to make their savage descents upon the northern islands and counties of Scotland. These sea-kings and their crews were for generations the terror of Western Europe. Fearless alike either of storm or foe, they swept down upon the seaboard of Caithness to ravage and destroy. Towns and villages were sacked and burnt, and the inhabitants scattered, slain, or carried into slavery. With graphic touch the poet thus pictures to us one of these sea-kings,

> " From out his castle on the strand
>   He led his tawny-bearded band
>   In stormy bark from land to land.
>
> " The red dawn was his goodly sign,
>   He set his face to sleet and brine,
>   And quaffed the blast like ruddy wine.
>
> " The storm-blast was his deity ;
>   His lover was the fitful sea ;
>   The wailing winds his melody.
>
> " By rocky scaur and beachy head
>   He followed where his fancy led,
>   And down the rainy waters fled,
>
> " And left the peopled towns behind,
>   And gave his days and nights to find
>   What lay beyond the western wind."

By-and-by the Vikings entirely changed their policy and tactics. They came, not to raid and depart again, but to remain and colonise. They acted the part of the camel who asked room in a tent for his head, and then, forcing his whole body in, dispossessed the inhabitants. The Norsemen founded settlements here and there on the coast, and ere long pressed the old Celtic inhabitants backward further and further into the interior. Thus did they leave to the former possessors only a strip of country parallel with the march of Sutherlandshire. Between the two races there was a border land, but no fixed boundary stone. Even to this day we can roughly define the extent and limits of the Scandinavian conquest and occupation by the Norse names on the northern and eastern side of the line, and the Celtic on the western and southern. To a keenly observant eye the distinction is visible in the prevailing physical type, for those of Viking blood may be known

> " By the tall form, blue eye, proportion fair,
> The limbs athletic, and the long light hair."

The contrast may also be noted in the character and habits of the two races; and there are many evidences of it in their language, and some even in their music. As to the last named element, it is worthy of note, and may surprise some people to know, that the bagpipe is rarely to be heard in Caithness. No doubt it is an ancient and honourable instrument, for a high authority has declared,

> " And Music first on earth was heard
> In Gaelic accents deep,
> When Jubal in his oxter squeezed
> The blether o' a sheep ; "

but in the Scandinavian county it is an exotic—an imported article from Sutherland—and little esteemed by the sons and daughters of the Norsemen. As a consequence of these statements I hope one excellent result will appear. We hear some people, for whom we entertain the sincerest pity, express in very vehement language their abhorrence of the bagpipe. In most cases this is no more than a proud pretence, but they have now an opportunity of proving their sincerity. If they like the north, but dislike the bagpipes, let them go to Caithness, and the nearer to John o' Groat's the better. As soon as this book is afloat, I shall expect to hear of a great demand for summer lodgings in the county. Please avoid the towns, however, for they are at times tainted with the Celtic musical element.

These statements regarding the people of Caithness would hardly be considered up to date were I to omit mention of two other circumstances. While the large majority of the inhabitants are of Scandinavian blood, there does exist a considerable Celtic element, due not so much to the remaining descendants of the old race, but still more to the scores and scores of families who were driven out of Sutherland early in this century by the cruel policy of eviction. These very naturally settled for the most part in the parishes nearest to their native county, among people many of whom were of their own blood and language. Of Saxon blood also there are undoubtedly some traces among the families of Caithness. Methinks I now hear some ignorant Southerner express his wonder that any one of Saxon lineage, and therefore

knowing better things, should wander and settle so far
north, even for gold or for love. It might be sufficient
to reply that his wonder will not diminish either the fact
or its significance. But we have a better instrument of
retort within reach. In this connection I cannot resist
the temptation to refer to a common reproach and a
delusion connected therewith. It has sometimes been
said in the south that "no fools come from Scotland,"
because those who in point of fact leave Scotland show
themselves wise by so doing. That being so, the number
of Scotsmen who have found their way to England is
supposed to be, to say the least of it, remarkably large.
Now I have a nice little fact to offer as a gift to our
English friends. It is asserted, and has, I believe, been
proved, that in proportion to the population of the two
countries, there are more Englishmen resident in Scotland
than Scotsmen resident in England. It is sometimes
quite delightful to make that statement to a typical
John Bull, and to watch its effect. If that dose appears
not to be sufficient, you may add this other, that, according to the same proportion, Scotland is, when tested
by taxation, the richest country in the world. One can
take a malicious pleasure in driving these points home
upon the class of " small " southerners, if they are at all
disposed to crow over " poor Scotland."

Had space permitted, I might here review the forma-
tive influences, such as natural scenery, social conditions
and institutions, history, and religion, which made the
Norsemen what they were, and have to so large an
extent moulded the people of Caithness into what they

are. With a bare and simple statement I must pass from that tempting theme. As compared with the Celts and the Saxons, the sons of the Vikings are characterised by restless energy, sturdy independence, singular adaptability, and frank generosity. When we remember that the inhabitants of our whole eastern seaboard, from John o' Groat's at least as far as the mouth of the Humber, are tinged with the same blood, we can understand how great has been the Norse influence in the formation of the British character, and how many and manifest its results in our national history and development.

Here I might be tempted to indulge at some length in a dissertation on the origin and fortunes of the family— for, strictly speaking, it should not be a clan—to which I have the honour to belong. These are matters of quite peculiar interest to me, but I have at least one good reason for reticence and brevity. So far as the far past is concerned, I should scarcely be able to say much to the credit of my ancestors. Even were I able to produce evidence of high character and noble deeds on the part of some of my " forbears," I should be checked by the salutary warning that

"They who on glorious ancestry enlarge,
Produce their debt instead of their discharge."

The truth is that my case very much resembles that of Sydney Smith, of whom some one inquired as to the decease of one of his progenitors. In reply, the humourist made the significant confession, " Well, he disappeared suddenly at the time of the assizes, and we asked no questions." If not quite so dark as is hinted at in these neatly-chosen words, the history of the Sinclairs is for the most part a record of rapine, blood, and strife, and any little traits or incidents of a more pleasing kind are only

"rari nantes in gurgite vasto."

It is said that on one occasion Columba, the noble missionary of Iona, was asked to invoke a blessing on a warrior's sword. He responded in the remarkable words, "God grant that it may never drink a drop of blood." Not for many generations was such a prayer uttered, or at least its burden fulfilled, in the case of a Sinclair's sword. They fought with every clan who dared to claim an inch of soil in Caithness, and appear at more than one period to have possessed the whole county. They were, however, most unfortunate when they ventured on expeditions far away from home. *How* wofully unfortunate they were, the more prominent chapters in their history will show! I shall only mention two instances.

The first of these takes us back into the early part of the sixteenth century. James IV. of Scotland had quarrelled with his brother-in-law, Henry VIII., and set out with a large army for the invasion of England. The Scotch army encamped upon the hill of Flodden, and on its northern slopes was fought, in 1513, the blackest battle in the annals of the northern kingdom. William Sinclair, Earl of Caithness, and 300 of his men were on the right wing of James's array, and even after others had fled from the scene of disaster fought to the bitter end. It almost looked like the extinction of

"The lordly line of high St Clair,"

for the Earl fell on the field, and scarcely a man—
perhaps not one at all—returned to tell the tale. When
leaving home on that fatal occasion the Sinclairs had worn
a green uniform, and had crossed the lofty ridge of the Ord,
the southern boundary of the county, on a Monday. Ever
since it has been an unwritten law that no one of the
name should ever wear that luckless colour, or cross the
Ord on the same unpropitious day of the week. Well
might the Sinclairs of Caithness at that date join in the
pathetic lament,

> "Dool for the order sent our lads to the Border,
>   The English for ance by guile wan the day ;
> The Flowers of the Forest that fought aye the foremost,
>   The prime of our land lie cauld on the clay.
>
> " We'll hae nae mair liltin' at the ewe milkin',
>   Women and bairns are heartless and wae ;
> Sighin' and moanin' on ilka green loanin',
>   The Flowers of the Forest are a' wede away."

The second great misfortune to the Sinclairs took place
about a century later, in 1612, during the war of young
Gustavus Adolphus against Norway and Denmark.
Colonel George Sinclair crossed to Norway with a force
variously estimated at from 300 to 1400 men, but most
probably about 900, with the intention of finding his way
over the mountains to Sweden. These troops were levied
" on the sly," and the " root of all evil " was not wanting
in the project. The Scotch king and government did
what they could to prevent its execution, and threatened
that the leaders would be " put to the horn," that is,
declared to be outlaws after three blasts of the horn at

the cross of Edinburgh. When Sinclair and his men landed in the Romsdal Fiord, they met with unexpected and serious resistance. They were attacked in a narrow defile in Gudbrandsdalen by large bodies of the peasantry, who, at a critical spot, hurled great masses of rock down upon them. Colonel Sinclair fell among the rest, and at least half his men were slain. Next day upwards of 100 more were put to death ; and only some eighteen escaped with their lives. A monument on the high road below the scene of conflict marks the grave of the leader, who was a son of John, the Master of Caithness, of whom we have by-and-bye an even more tragic story to tell. The people of Norway are proud of their victory over the Sinclairs, and it has frequently been made the subject of song. Here are the first and last verses of a free translation of one of these ballads :—

> " To Norway Sinclair steered his course
>   Across the salt sea wave,
>   But in Kringelen's mountain pass
>   He found an early grave.
>   To fight for Swedish gold he sailed,
>   He and his hireling band :
>   Help, God ; and nerve the peasant's arm
>   To wield the patriot brand.
>
> . . . .
>
> "Oh many a maid and mother wept
>   And father's cheek grew pale,
>   When from the few survivors' lips
>   Was heard the startling tale.
>   A monument yet marks the spot
>   Which points to Sinclair's bier,
>   And tells how fourteen hundred men
>   Sunk in that pass of fear."

In justice to my clansmen, I must here take leave to

repel an insinuation, and also to correct an error. In some accounts of the fatal expedition, and especially in a ballad by one called Storm, the Sinclairs are represented as having burnt and plundered wherever they went. They are even accused of having slain children at their mothers' breasts. All this is absolutely untrue. One Envold Kruse, a local stadtholder, reporting officially on the subject, says, "We have also since ascertained that those Scots who were defeated and captured on their march through this country, have absolutely neither burnt, murdered, nor destroyed anything." Again, in the last verse quoted above, the number of Colonel Sinclair's band is stated at 1400 men. Space would fail me to enter fully into a discussion of these figures. This, however, after careful and exhaustive investigation by competent authorities, may be held as proven, that the Caithness men cannot have been more than 900 at the utmost, and that 500 is probably nearer the correct figure.

As a foil, though but a partial one, to these stories of disaster, it may be well to note one of the Sinclair chiefs, who was a distinguished patriot and soldier. This was Sir William Sinclair, who played his part so bravely at the battle of Bannockburn that King Robert the Bruce, in acknowledgment of his valorous exploits, presented him with a beautiful sword. On the broad blade was inscribed this legend: "Le Roi me donne, St Clair me porte," *i.e.*, The king gifts me, St Clair carries me. At a later date, the gallant knight again showed his devotion to his monarch. Before he died, King Robert charged

Lord James of Douglas to have his heart embalmed, carefully borne to the Holy Land, and finally deposited in the Holy Sepulchre. After the king's decease, Sir William Sinclair was one of the knights who set out with Douglas on his pious errand to Palestine ; but he fell, as Douglas himself did not very long after, in an encounter with the Moors in Spain.

Before coming to more modern times and more civilised ways, let me here insert two weird old stories, the scenes of which are in different parts of the county. One at least of these is undoubtedly founded on fact, though over what is true not a little that is mythical and imaginative has grown, like the lichen on the lettering of an old tombstone. It is neither my business nor my intention to attempt to disentangle these elements ; and, therefore, I shall present the traditions just as they have shaped themselves in my memory, after somewhat careful inquiry and study.

The first, and perhaps the more doubtful of these, which I shall make also the briefer, is a story of the Bruan coast, some ten miles south of Wick. Nowhere, even on the Caithness seaboard, are the rocks and caves and goes more fantastically wild and imposing. Only those who have sailed along beneath their shadows know their varied and marvellous attractions. It is not, however, with these that we have at present to do.

At a particular spot on this iron-bound coast, there is a bold rock or cliff, which the Gaelic people call " Leac na oir," *i.e.*, the rock of gold. The traveller will easily find a civil and obliging Bruan man to point out its situation. The story connected with that rock and its name is one of treachery and cruelty. For a moment I thought of calling it also a story of love, but the sequel will show why that word has been omitted. A Caithness chieftain, probably a Sinclair, though I hope not, seems to have possessed lands and a residence on this coast. He had wooed and won a Danish lady or Princess, but we have no record of their courtship, if, indeed, anything of the kind ever took place. She seems, however, to have consented to make Caithness her adopted home. At length, the time of the marriage drew near, and it was decided that the ceremony should take place on this side the North Sea. Embarking in a Danish vessel, she sailed for the land of her adoption, and might surely hope for an affectionate welcome from her lover. She certainly did not come empty-handed, for the vessel bore the lady's splendid dowry of gold and treasure. But alas! what a fickle, treacherous, cruel creature is man, though he be a Caithnessman, or even a Sinclair! The chieftain was more in love with the dowry than with the lady. Under pretence of securing her safety, it had been arranged that a bright light should be exhibited on the coast, toward which the Danes might with confidence steer their vessel. The greedy, heartless lover fixed that light purposely on the most dangerous cliff he could select, and the result, unfortunately, was entirely in accordance with his fell design. At dead of night, when not a glimmer of light shone in the sky, the bride's vessel struck the fatal rock, and in a few brief moments, falling back in shattered fragments, sunk beneath the waves. The Danish lady and her convoy perished with the wreck, for not a hand was extended to rescue them. The chieftain roared with delight at this primary success of his project, but most probably did not after all gain his ultimate end. In his day it would be no easy matter, if, indeed, possible at all, to fish up the gold and other treasure from among the seaweed and rocks. We should all be sorry to think that the wretch was made one penny the richer by the spoils. Let us hope that they still lie among the

> " Wedges of gold, great anchors, heaps of pearl,
> Inestimable stones, unvalued jewels,
> All scattered in the bottom of the sea."

If even now the Danish gold and jewellery are there, we shall leave them undisturbed in the spirit of the poetess who sings—

> " Yet more, the depths have more ! what wealth untold,
> Far down, and shining through their stillness, lies !
> Thou hast the starry gems, the burning gold,
> Won from ten thousand royal argosies !
> Sweep o'er thy spoils, thou wild and wrathful main !
> Earth claims not *these* again ! "

Of the many ruined castles which stud the cliffs of Caithness, the Sinclairs once possessed the great majority, for most of them belonged to one branch or other of that powerful family. Probably one of the oldest of these is the venerable Castle of Keiss, on the western shore of Sinclair Bay,—a ruin indeed, yet how stately and firm on its rocky basement. Its main walls are still wonderfully entire, and its lofty turrets and gables are visible far over land and sea. On the opposite side of the same

spacious bay, and crowning cliffs of wild grandeur, stand
the twin Castles Sinclair and Girnigoe, the chief stronghold of the Earls of Caithness in the old days of blood
and iron.   The very image of that grim and gaunt
fastness recalls the questions and replies of Heine's
song—

" Hast thou seen the castle olden,
  High towering by the sea ?
Crimson—bright and golden
  The clouds above it be.

Down stooping, it appeareth
  In the glassy wave below ;
Its lofty towers it reareth
  Where the clouds of even glow.

Well have I seen it towering
  That castle by the sea ;
And the moon above it lowering,
  And the mists about it flee.

The winds and waves rebounding—
  Say, rang they fresh and clear ?
Heard'st thou from bright halls sounding
  Music and festal cheer ?

The winds and waves were sleeping,
  But from that castle high
The sound of wailing and weeping
  Brought tears into my eye."

Castles Sinclair and Girnigoe are perched on a bold,
rocky promontory which runs out almost parallel with
the cliffs of the mainland, a deep, wild goe rocking its
surging waters between.   Castle Sinclair, the more modern and yet the more ruinous, stands on the neck of the
projecting cape ; while Castle Girnigoe, the older and

yet the more perfect, occupies the crown of the rock, and its walls seem at one time to have extended far beyond the present structure. The twin strongholds may be said to have a joint tenancy of the peninsula, and once-a-day a drawbridge over a yawning gulf connected their walls and chambers. Far out upon the point of the cliffs where they first dip downward toward the sea, are the remains of an *oubliette* or secret dungeon. Thence, through a trap door, and by a steep slide on the face of the rocks, communication might be had with the waters and boats below.

On the ground floor of Castle Girnigoe, three or four separate chambers yet remain in a fair state of preservation. From a corner in one of these, a flight of broken steps leads down to a damp, vaulted dungeon, dimly lit from a narrow aperture in the wall. This was the scene of the terrible tragedy, of which we must presently tell the sad history. If ruins could feel or manifest the sense of shame, then surely, Girnigoe! thou mightest well blush even in thine old age!

> " Yet, proudly mid the tide of years,
>   Thou lift'st on high thine airy form
> Scene of primeval hopes and fears,
>   Slow yielding to the storm ! "

Certainly, if Goethe be right in describing architecture as petrified music, Castles Sinclair and Girnigoe sound out one of the most gruesome dirges or laments that was ever embodied in stone.

About the middle of the sixteenth century, George Sinclair, Earl of Caithness, became bitterly incensed against his eldest son, John, the Master of Caithness and his father's heir. The cause of disagreement has been variously stated. According to one account, the Earl had a bitter feud with the inhabitants of Dornoch in Sutherlandshire, and had sent his son, along with the chief of the clan Mackay, to punish them. The towns-people had promised certain concessions, and had given three hostages as a pledge of their fidelity. The angry, treacherous Earl ordered these men to be executed forth-with. His son, and Mackay of Strathnaver—to their credit be it said—refused to carry out his decision, and so the rupture took place between them and him. The young Master, to escape the anger and resentment of his father, took refuge with his ally Mackay in the Reay country, and resided there for several years. This absence from home gave rise to two other causes of offence and sus-picion. In the first place, rumours from time to time reached the Earl that his son and Mackay were plotting against him, and even cherished designs against his life. Moreover, as in many such cases, we must have regard to the counsel, "Cherchez la femme;" and in this instance, it will yield something. The chief of the Mackays had, it is said, a charming daughter, who quite captived the Earl's son, and eventually became his wife. This gave great offence to his father, who, being by this time a widower, was himself contemplating matrimony again. He resented the idea of his son's outstripping him, and first becoming the father of another heir to the earldom. Moved by these or such like causes of offence, the Earl, who was naturally jealous and cruel, laid a plot to ensnare both his rebellious son and his traditional enemy at once. He invited them to come to Castle Girnigoe, and professed the most sincere anxiety to be reconciled to them both.

Trusting to the Earl's good faith, they rode together, on horseback and unattended, to the fatal towers on Sinclair Bay. As they were entering by the drawbridge, the Chief of the Mackays noticed what he considered an unusual and unnecessary force of armed men on duty. Taking alarm at once, he turned his horse's head on the very bridge, and fled with all speed. The young Master was, however, less fortunate. He was at once seized and thrust down into the damp and gloomy cell in the under regions of Girnigoe; and there he lay, in cruel neglect and solitude, for many years. His first keeper was one Murdo Roy, who planned the escape of his young and gallant prisoner. The plot was discovered by William, the Earl's second son, and Murdo was summarily executed for his kindly intentions toward his ward. His head for some time after adorned the castle walls. A short time after poor Murdo's fate was thus sealed, William entered the prisoner's cell, and the brothers had an angry altercation. At length John, who was a man of powerful physique, and therefore called *Garrow*, the strong, sprang, fettered though he was, upon his brother, and actually crushed his life out in an iron embrace. It is but right to add that William had espoused his father's side, had threatened his brother's life, and would not have been much grieved to have the heir out of his way.

During these events the Earl was absent from home,

but immediately on his return, he appointed two keepers, by name James and Ingram Sinclair, to watch the young Master, so that he was guarded more carefully and treated more cruelly than ever. As to the part latterly played by these gaolers, traditions differ. According to one story, they plundered the castle in the Earl's absence, fled with the spoils, and left the Master of Caithness to perish of famine in his cell. Another version, more circumstantial, and, alas! far more revolting, seems unfortunately the true one, or at least nearer to the sad truth. It is said that the two Sinclairs, instigated by the Earl himself, deliberately compassed the death of the poor captive—and that by a most inhuman method. Having starved their victim for a few days, they then set before him an abundant supply of salt beef, of which he ate voraciously. Then, when raging thirst came upon him, they refused him even a drop of water, and left him to die in writhing agony. The inscription on his tombstone in the old churchyard of Wick, speaks of him as " ane noble and worthie man, who departed this life the 15th day of March, 1576."

The old Earl, the father, died in Edinburgh in 1583, and was succeeded by George, the son of the murdered Master. This George very soon took opportunity to avenge his father's death upon the brothers Sinclair. One of them, Ingram, was to be married, and the new Earl, to make his vengeance the more terrible, chose the wedding day for his purpose. He first met James, who was making his way to the happy festivities, ran him through with his sword, and left him a corpse by the roadside. Proceeding yet further on his bloody errand, he found Ingram with some companions beguiling the time before the ceremony in a game of football. The Earl approached him at once, saying, in a tone of cheery innocence, " Do you know, one of my corbies (*i.e.*, crows, a familiar name for pistols) missed fire this morning ? " At the same moment, as if to examine it, he drew a pistol from the holster on his saddle, and shot the bridegroom dead upon the spot. Instead of a happy bridal came a double funeral, and no one was bold enough or strong enough " to bell the cat," and bring the Earl to justice. It may even have been thought that he was fully justified in wreaking vengeance on the men who so cruelly murdered his father. These were not the days of long-spun, wearisome trials. The whole story is but a specimen of many such deeds and scenes in the old days in Caithness ; let us hope that the one now recorded is the most unnatural and inhuman of all. If any one thinks that such things never have been done, and never could be done, south of the Grampians, let him turn to the year 1402, in the kingdom of Fife, and find out what became of the Duke of Rothesay, the King's son, in the palace of Falkland. Two blacks do not make a white ; but the question here is, which is the deeper black, and, really, there seems little to choose between the two cases.

More than perhaps any other county in Scotland, Caithness has, during the past thirty years especially, been passing through stage after stage of rapid transition, almost amounting to revolution. This is true in regard to politics, social conditions, and religious questions alike.

K

Public opinion and sentiment have undergone changes, the pace of which has become more and more rapid every year. Some of "the adorers of time gone by" have been weeping and wailing profusely. My own opinion is, that in these changes there has been much to regret, but far far more to cause rejoicing. It is not my purpose here to discuss the pros and cons of these various currents in the minds of men. Two things, however, I think I may do without offence, namely, state in a few words some of the motive causes of change and offer a few slight illustrations of the contrast between the dead or dying past and the living present.

Among the active forces which have caused upheaval, four seem to me to be the most powerful and prominent. These are, the spread of education, railway extension, the wider diffusion of press influence, and the pressure of hard times as regards the harvests both of land and sea. Only on the first of these shall I venture to speak ; and though sorely tempted to write chapters, I must restrain personal feeling and impulse, and be content with a few sentences. Education was, without doubt, the first of the forces of change to operate upon Caithness. Fifty years ago, there were many shrewd and prosperous men in the county, whose training, even in the three R's—Reading, Riting, and Rithmetic—was very imperfect indeed. Let me instance one rather amusing case. It was that of a shoemaker who provided the Sheriff of the county with boots. The worthy tradesman had with no little trouble and pains drawn up an account to be presented to his customer ; yet, when it was

completed, he found, to his chagrin, that he could not
read it himself. Once and again he had made the
attempt and failed; but at length a happy thought gave
him immediate relief and comfort. Turning to a friend,
he exclaimed, with a satisfied smile, " Weel, I canna
mak't oot, but d— cares, it's gaun til a better scholar
than masel." What a comfort to know that the Sheriff
could read so well. Such is the story. Even thirty
years ago such a case must have been somewhat rare in
the county. At that time the schools of the county
were admirably taught, and the standard of education
wonderfully high. As one evidence for the truth of
these statements, I may mention that at that period,
Caithness sent to Edinburgh more students in proportion to her population than any other county in Scotland,
with the possible exception of Dumfries. There is also
one rural parish which may, without fear of rivalry,
claim as natives a larger number of professional men
scattered all over the world than, perhaps, any other
in the country. This general diffusion of sound and
well advanced education paved the way for the breaking up of many an old tradition and sentiment embedded
in the life of the community. Thus has it come to pass
that in many questions affecting especially the Church
and the land, " the axles are so hot that we have long
been smelling fire." To vary the figure we may say
that what an eminent statesman lately called " the
invisible creeping wind of public sentiment " has been
blowing about many old leaves.

In the regions of social life and of politics, it may be

of interest to chronicle some forms or aspects of change, even though I refrain from pronouncing any opinion upon them.

Among what are called the middle classes, the humble and homely ways of half a century ago are fast passing away. Contentment and simplicity are more rarely found, while pride and luxury are manifesting themselves in growing measure. Some one has contrasted these conditions in the following plain and pithy lines :—

> " Man to the plough,
>   Wife to the sow,
>   Son to the flail,
>   Daughter to the pail,
>   And your rents will be netted ;
>   But man tally-ho,
>   Daughter piano,
>   Son Greek and Latin,
>   Wife silk and satin,
>   And you'll soon be gazetted."

Very sorry should I be to apply these words to the middle-class people of Caithness as a whole. Still, they indicate, in an exaggerated and therefore harmless form, the direction in which things are tending. Let us hope that in no case will the sad end with which the lines close be realised. If we look a step lower in the social scale, what do we find ? Among the small farmers and crofters the changes in progress have been not so much in social condition, for that as yet has been little altered, but in political feeling and aspiration. Twenty or thirty years ago, the minds of these men were as to great questions in a listless, almost stagnant, condition.

Within the last decade the land question has set the heather on fire, and burns on hundreds if not thousands of hearths in the valleys and villages of Caithness. What many would call a social rebellion smoulders all over the county, and there are not so many now-a-days disposed to echo the pious wish :—

> " Bless the squire and his relations,
>   And keep us all in our proper stations."

It is an undoubted fact—welcome it or bewail it, which-ever you please—that Radicalism more or less extreme is rampant in almost every parish.

Not less real though perhaps less patent are the changes in religious thought and customs. Into these I cannot fully enter, but I may gather as from the surface of things a few indications of the contrast between the *then* of fifty years ago and the *now* of 1890. Nowhere in all Scotland did there exist at the earlier period a more dogged and determined conservatism in matters religious than in Caithness. As to outward forms many would sing, *con amore*,

> " Old customs !   Oh I love the sound !
>   However simple they may be ;
> Whate'er with time hath sanction found
>   Is welcome and is dear to me."

It is the fashion with some people to stigmatize that spirit in unmeasured terms as if it were only and wholly evil —the fruit of nothing but tyranny and ignorance. Those who so speak show on their own part a want of know-ledge no less than of breadth and charity. Among many things which seem to most of us grotesque and foolish, the candid eye can take note of many things which were good and noble. It is therefore in no carping or jeering spirit that I touch upon the lighter side of some phenomena in religious life which are now little more than memories.

Among the good folks of Caithness half a century ago the office of the Christian ministry commanded a singular measure of deference and respect. This was due to the character both of the office itself and of the men, generally speaking, who discharged its duties. There were, for example, certain amusements which might be permissible or barely so among ordinary Christians, but which were not to be tolerated for a moment in one of "the cloth." You remember the cynical charge addressed by Sydney Smith to a young clergyman:

> "Hunt not, fish not, shoot not,
> Dance not, fiddle not, flute not;
> Be sure you have nothing to do with the Whigs,
> But stay at home and feed your pigs;
> Above all, I make it my particular desire
> That at least once a week you dine with the Squire."

The first six counsels at all events are in full accordance with the common opinion of religious people in the far north at that period. Any man who practised such things would be denounced and boycotted by those who were reputed the best of the people. Exception, however, was made in favour—if so it can be called—of the "moderate" ministers. They were considered so hopelessly wrong in other respects that no one cared to criticise too nicely any questionable thing they might do.

A curious incident bearing upon this point occurred in the case of the famous "Apostle of the North," Dr John Macdonald of Ferintosh. Some details may have escaped my memory, but I believe that what follows is in the main correct. His father, James Macdonald, was catechist in the parish of Reay, and was a man of high religious repute. His son John was born in the depth of winter, and the father carried his child through wreaths of snow to the manse that he might be baptized. The minister was from home; he had gone out shooting with the laird; but the catechist, nothing daunted and bearing his tender load, went in pursuit over the snowy moors, and at length, after no little labour, came up with his pastor. The ceremony was performed there and then, simply and briefly. Stepping out upon a frozen sheet of water, the minister broke a hole in the ice, lifted the all but frozen element between his fingers, and dropped it on the child's face with the usual formula. That boy became the wonderful preacher of after years, and often with pawky humour declared that his baptism was but a foretaste of the cold treatment he ever after received at the hands of the "Moderates." No evangelical who cared for his good name and influence would go shooting with the laird, and have to be hunted in such a fashion.

Since godly ministers were held in such high estimation, curious results sometimes followed. Young preachers were tempted to imitate the old; and, as usual, what they reproduced was often the very faults or foibles of the model. The most remarkable thing is that at times a young man was highly thought of because there was some resemblance in his person or manner to a very weakness or oddity of a greater than himself. A highly respected minister in Caithness, about the year 1830, was the Rev. Archibald Cook of Bruan, who was commonly spoken of as Archie Cook. He was a man of deep piety and quaint genius, but was also peculiar and somewhat eccentric. In his day, a young man, newly fledged, preached in a Caithness Church. After service, there were many comments on his performance—mostly of an unfavourable kind. One good old woman, however, abounding in Christian charity, found out one peculiar excellence at least in the neophyte. Being asked by a neighbour what she thought of him, she at once replied,

"Oh, wumman,'am thinkan he's a rayal godly, gracious young man. He coughs jist like Airchie Cook."

I have even been assured that the qualification mentioned was the means of his appointment as pastor over that very congregation. It may not be wise to show any countenance to such a view, for it might produce effects at which one shudders among the rising ministry. We do not wish to find in the pulpit analogies of infinite variety to the Alexandra limp or Archie Cook's cough.

If in these old days the ministers were carefully fenced in by restraints in one direction, so were the people by laws and statutes in others. Here, however, I must confess that I go back more than two hundred years for my illustration. It appears that, even at that early period, the offence of non-church-going was sadly prevalent. If so, it was not for lack of strong enactments on the subject. Here is an extract from the Session Records of the parish of Canisbay :—

"December 27, 1652.—Ordained ꝩt (y for th, or the, all through) for mending ye people, ye better to keepe ye Kirk, a roll of ye names of ye families be taken up, and Sabbathlie, yt they be called upon by name, and who bees notted absent sall pay 40d. *toties quoties.*" The last two words simply mean that " as often," as the offence was committed, "so often" should the penalty be inflicted. The worthy minister who first quoted this extract fifty years ago, touchingly remarks, " This is a most salutary regulation." I believe that, even down to his day, the law *might* have been enforced : who would dare to attempt it now ? But mark, I pray you, what a wistful, plaintive ring there is about the minister's declaration. Can the 40d. have anything to do with it ? How the stipends and spirits of ministers would mount up, and the coffers of the Churches bulge out, if such a source of revenue could be tapped in this wealthy but degenerate nineteenth century ! No wonder many good people in this world are adorers of the past ! Must 1 add a line more ? No wonder that many more profanely prefer the present !

An old custom, not yet extinct, but fast losing its hold, was the " reading of the line " in the public service of praise. As some may not understand that expression, it may be well to state its meaning. When the minister " gave out " several verses of a Psalm to be sung, the precentor proceeded to read aloud the first line

with strong intonation, and then led the congregation in
singing it. He then read the second line in the same
fashion, and again led off the volume of united praise ;
and so on with each line of the verses announced from
the pulpit. The practice probably originated in the fact
that many worshippers in the Highlands were unable to
read either their own or any other language. In that
case, it served the useful purpose of enabling all to join
in the praises of the sanctuary. Through those congregations in which the services were conducted in Gaelic,
the "reading of the line" became common in Caithness,
even in those parishes where the English language was the
medium of worship. No stranger can have any idea of
the importance attached to this custom in the north. It
has been adhered to with the utmost tenacity, and dies
hard. When attempts have been made in certain
parts of the country to secure its abandonment, bitter
wrangling and sometimes even serious disruption in
congregations have been the consequence. The "reading of the line" has even been accounted an essential in
spiritual worship, and any word or action tending to its
disparagement has been regarded as nothing less than
sacrilege. Some who can see nothing either specially
good or specially evil in the practice may be disposed to
ask on what grounds its sacred character has been supposed to rest. That question I cannot fully answer, but
this I do know, that it has sometimes been defended on
grounds of Scripture. The words in the prophecy of
Isaiah, "line upon line, line upon line" have been
quoted as an argument and warrant for the practice.

It is not likely that the custom will long survive unless provided with some better defence.

The false interpretation put upon the prophet's words is no better and no worse than another of which I have heard. A very different application of the passage was once made not many miles from Grangemouth in Stirlingshire. Two brothers called Little—please note the name—possessed a small property in that district. They were bachelors, and, perhaps, a little lonely, so upon one occasion they invited both the parish minister and the parish schoolmaster to dinner. The brothers occupied opposite ends of the table, while the two guests sat *vis-a-vis* at the sides. During dinner, or more probably towards its close, the elder brother took up the prophet's words, and applied them skilfully to the group around the table. Extending his left hand toward the schoolmaster, he said, " Line upon line ; " reaching out his right toward the minister, he said, " precept upon precept ; " touching his own breast, he said, " here a *Little* ; " pointing across to his brother, he said, " and there a *Little*." In Caithness the " reading of the line " is to a large extent a thing of the past. Improved education and taste are both against it, and its days are numbered.

Before closing this chapter, it may be noted that among the old ministers and people of Caithness, quiet humour was both displayed and appreciated. Moreover, it was not considered out of place in its moderate application even to sacred things. There is, I know, one clergyman still alive and much respected in Caithness,

who could supply many choice illustrations of the truth
of what I have said.   Many have long wished he would
give them to the public.   Those who like myself are
natives of the county, but have lived very little in it,
must be content with small store of these sweet morsels.
Let me offer one or two out of the small stock I possess.

It has always been a marked characteristic of the
religious people of Caithness, that they made large use of
Scripture language and illustration even in the affairs of
everyday life.   This arose from no irreverence, but from
the strong hold which the sacred diction had taken of
their minds.   Their speech was saturated with the words
and phrases of Holy Writ.   On one occasion two or
three of " the Men " came to visit my father at the
manse.   It may be well to mention for the information
of some readers, that these pious laymen of religious
repute and influence were called " Men," as some one
has said, " not because they were not women, but
because they were not ministers."   They were elders of
the Church and leaders of the people in spiritual
matters.   Well, a few of them came from a considerable
distance, and knocked at the kitchen door of the manse.
The servant invited them to enter, provided them with
seats, and asked what message she would carry to her
master.   One of them, speaking for   all, gave   this
peculiar reply.   " Tell 'im 'e be keepan' 'is picklies o'
whate because 'e Midianites hev come."   When the girl
delivered her message, my father's smile told that he
understood its meaning perfectly and at once, and he
went downstairs immediately to give his visitors a

cordial welcome. Perhaps I should repeat the words in a form intelligible to all. "Tell him to be keeping his pickles of wheat because the Midianites have come." Now, what did the message mean? In the book of Judges we read that Gideon "threshed wheat by the wine press, to hide it from the Midianites." So the worthy men, clothing their words in Scripture language, intended to say, "If the minister has any precious truths or experiences which he does not care to communicate to others, let him hide them, for we are like the Midianites—we shall steal them if we can." There is something far more than merely delicate humour in the story.

On one occasion a most worthy minister in the parish of Latheron offered to drive me as far as the Ord, the boundary headland of Caithness, on my way southward to Ross-shire. As we were passing Dunbeath, we overtook a somewhat doubtful-looking character, who asked if he might get a "lift," and assured us he would trespass on our kindness only for "a mile and no more."

"Come away, then," said Mr M., the minister, in a kindly tone; "get up behind."

On we went at a fair pace, and the mile was soon covered. Our new acquaintance kept up a lively conversation with the minister, whom he had at once recognised. By-and-bye the second mile was more than past, and he still kept his seat. At last Mr M. thought it high time to give the stranger a hint, and he did it with no less delicacy than humour.

"Do you know, friend," said the minister, "you have

reminded me very forcibly of one of the injunctions given by our Lord to His disciples ? "

" Indeed—indeed !—what was that ? " replied the stranger, much interested, and apparently gratified.

" Well," said Mr M., turning half round, " don't you remember the words, ' Whosoever shall compel thee to go a mile, go with him twain ? "

The stranger was silent for a little while, and then, evidently desiring to ponder the words alone, bade us a grateful " Good-bye," and stepped down from his seat.

The following are two illustrations from the sayings of eminent preachers belonging to Caithness. On a certain occasion one of these announced as his text the words in Revelation, " There was silence in heaven for the space of half-an-hour." He began his discourse by declaring, with much emphasis, " Well, friends, this is a sad intimation for the female portion of my congregation." It strikes me I have heard the same remark attributed to some southern divine. Perhaps I am wrong ; I shall be glad if my memory fails me in this particular. If two, or even more, have said it, may it not be because great minds often arrive without any collusion at the same important conclusion ?

Another Caithness minister was once discoursing on the duty of Christians to " wash one another's feet." Here is a quaint extract from the sermon—taken down however, before the days of shorthand.

" One way in which disciples wash one another's feet is by reproving one another. But the reproof must not be couched in angry words, so as to destroy the effect ; nor in tame, so as to fail of effect. It must be just as in washing a brother's feet—you must not use boiling water to scald, nor frozen water to freeze them."

Some of the ministers of Caithness in these old days were narrow in opinion, severe in censure, arbitrary in rule, and harsh in doctrine ; but most of them were also men of genuine piety, much kindliness of heart, and warm hospitality ; a few at least bore the stamp of lofty genius. They " served their generation "—they were not sent or meant to serve ours ; and as a body they deserved the high respect in which they were held by the people.

CHAPTER VI.

THE TOWN OF THURSO.

THURSO is the most northern town on the mainland of Great Britain. The origin of the name I hold to be still uncertain, and am prepared to give my reasons. Will my readers join me in a short excursion into the region of etymology ? There are two derivations given of the word Thurso—the one Scandinavian, the other Celtic. Naturally, I should prefer the former, but there are circumstances about the latter which stagger me. What are these rival views ? Let me first present the case from the Norse aspect. The original form of the name, according to many, was *Thorsaa*, that is, *Thor's aa*, which means *Thor's river*. From the stream the name passed to the town, and thence in later times to the Bay. It thus appears that from a very early period the river and town were under the protection of Thor, the son of Odin the supreme being, and, therefore, the second in rank of the Scandinavian deities. Being the most valiant among them, he acted the part of defender and avenger of all the other gods. His great weapon was a mallet or hammer, which, as often as he discharged it, returned to his hand again. He also wore a girdle, which had the peculiar virtue of renewing his strength again when he

From Photo. by G. W. Wilson.

THE CLETT ROCK, HOLBORN HEAD, THURSO.

was faint or weary. This was the tutelary deity of Thurso.

Now for the Celtic view of the question. The Gaelic name of Thurso is *Bal-inver-Horsa*, that is, the town of the river-mouth of Horsa, or sometimes simply *Inver-Horsa*, the river-mouth or landing place of Horsa. Now, Horsa is the name of a well-known Saxon warrior, who, along with his brother Hengist, defeated the Scots and Picts in a battle at Stamford in Lincolnshire. The question is, Had he ever any connection with Caithness? Old chronicles say he had. The story goes that Horsa and Hengist, with the son and nephew of the latter, sailed north in forty ships, and overran Caithness. Further, it is said that a great battle between them and the natives took place somewhere in the county. At this point a curious little piece of evidence comes in. In an appendix to "Pennant's Tour in Scotland in 1769," the Rev. Alexander Pope of Reay, a great antiquarian, says that in his parish "there is a place called *Tout Horsa*, or Horsa's grave, where they say that some great warrior was slain and buried; in the place is a great stone erected. Probably he was one of Horsa's captains." It is not easy to get over these names and statements; but I confess I should *like* to believe in the river-town of Thor.

The town was founded about the twelfth century, and was made a Burgh of Barony in 1633, by Charles the First. Several centuries ago, Thurso was a place of great commercial importance and carried on an extensive trade with Norway. Apparently King David believed in the honesty and justice of the Caithness people, for

L

the weights and measures of the county were made the standard for all his kingdom.   Here are the very words of the decree.   By the "Regiam Majestatem," chap. xiv., "It is statute be King David that ane comon and equal weicht quhilk (which) is called the weicht of Cathness— pondus Cathaniæ—in buying and selling, sall be keeped and vsed (used) be all men within this realm of Scotland."   It is said that the standards so set up by law belonged originally and properly to the town of Thurso. Now-a-days the commerce of Thurso is of comparatively little account, and the transference of County Courts and like business generally to Wick has given the former capital a somewhat deserted, or, as the inhabitants might say, dignified air.

The town, fifty or sixty years ago, consisted of three main parts.   Down by the river mouth and harbour lay a confused and crowded mass of poor dwellings, known as the "Fisher Biggings," that is, *buildings* of a humble type.   These were inhabited chiefly, as the name indicates, by fisher folks, with a sprinkling of the poorer class of labourers.   Behind this lowly district and at some distance from the river and shore, was the commercial portion of the town, with the busy shops and comfortable dwellings of the merchant class.   Behind these again, on yet more elevated levels, were the suburban residences of those who were credited with wealth or rank, among whom were bankers, lawyers, and county families.   To put the matter plainly, the inhabitants consisted of first, second, and third class passengers on the journey of life.   I have always thought of Thurso as a sort of modern and northern Capernaum. Down by the shore at the "Fisher Biggings" we might find toilers of the sea like the sons of Zebedee, and customs-men like Matthew the publican, while in the suburban homes might dwell wealthy Pharisees and Sadducees, and, let us hope, many liberal-minded philanthropists like the pious centurion. One thing more ere we pass from the town itself. It would be foolish in me to pronounce upon the rival merits of Wick or Thurso, for I hope to find readers in both towns. If you belong to the south of Scotland, you may understand their relations to one another when I say that Thurso is the Edinburgh and Wick the Glasgow of Caithness. A popular preacher some time ago very happily described the Scottish Capital as "an east - windy, west - endy" place. The description might very suitably be divided between the two northern towns, for if Wick is the east-windy, Thurso is the west-endy place. If the former is devoted to bustling commerce, the latter is a worshipper of

"That repose
Which stamps the caste of Vere de Vere."

Passing through the streets of Thurso, the visitor comes out upon an esplanade, built on the rocks which rise above the splendid sea-beach. Thence the view, northward across the Bay of Thurso to Holborn Head, and north-eastward across the Bay of Dunnet to the headland of the same name, can scarcely be surpassed on the Scottish coast. The Pentland Firth runs from point to point between the two bluff promontories, and toward the right the Orkney Islands close in the far horizon. On the western side of Hoy, the island nearest to Thurso, rises a remarkable thin pillar of rock, detached from the cliffs and rising high above them, to which the name of the " Old Man " has been applied.

> " See Hoy's Old Man, whose summit bare
> Pierces the dark blue fields of air ;
> Based in the sea, his fearful form
> Glooms like the spirit of the storm."

The great double bay—some four square miles in area—is almost entirely open to the north, but the two head-lands protect it from the east and west winds.

Strolling along the esplanade from the confines of the town, we reach the battered ruined remains of the Bishop's palace on the crown of a rocky projection high above the beach. This was the official residence of Bishop John, the story of whose cruel death we shall tell in due course. At some distance beyond these ruins, the bay turns abruptly toward the north and embraces the roadstead and harbour of Scrabster, the former a favourite shelter for vessels and the latter a busy little port. Thence the cliffs rise rapidly upward till they reach the lofty elevation of Holborn Head, where the waters of the broad bay are merged in the open swirling sea of the Pentland Firth. At the headland itself, and for a long distance beyond, the cliffs are most precipitous, and assume very impressive and often fantastic forms. There are deep goes with overhanging walls, hollow sounding caves from which come the frequent thuds of waves, grotesque bridges below which we catch glimpses of the surging, moaning waters beyond, and deep pits, edged round by the grassy sod, in whose abysses the waters crawl about and gurgle without ceasing. Opposite a wide recess in the rocky walls, there stands a lofty detached rock called the Clett—its overhanging sides crowned with a flat bonnet of green and its tiers of ledges dotted all over with multitudes of white sea-birds. This imposing stack was, according to his own story, the scene of an extraordinary exploit on the part of a Thurso "character." Whatever may be thought of the feat itself—we shall describe it by-and-bye—the scene of it was at least well chosen and quite sufficient for the purpose.

Such are some of the outward features of Thurso and the scenery in its neighbourhood. It is now my duty to deal with a very important matter affecting its reputation. The town has long lain under the burden of a singular and most serious reproach.

Now, as soon as I mention this subject, it is not at all unlikely that some of the modern inhabitants will at once be reminded of that noble and eloquent preacher, the Rev. Dr Thomas Guthrie, of Edinburgh, aye, and of world-wide fame. About thirty years ago, that eminent man, in addressing a church gathering of some sort, stated that in the town of Thurso, and when he himself was preaching, he had seen 600 people asleep in church. A great storm, of which no warning was given in any forecast, burst over Scotland immediately after, and, as was natural, raged most severely in the northern counties. The newspaper offices, even of Edinburgh, felt its effects for weeks after. Some said that the Rev. Doctor, though of course ignorantly and unintentionally, had told what was simply untrue. Others stood up boldly for the substantial accuracy of his statement, but were quite willing to accept 599 as the actual number. On one point there was practical unanimity. There may have been 600 whose heads were bowed down during the discourse ; but that did not settle the important question whether they were or were not asleep. Personally, I am of opinion that the Doctor did not make sufficient allowance either for the reverent demeanour of northern church audiences generally, or for the weighty importance of the theme of discourse, or for the overpowering effect of his own eloquence. Surely—to take the last point alone—he should have been glad to see 600 heads of wheat bowed before the persuasive breath of his oratory, like golden grain before the wind. On the whole, I think the people of Thurso did not come off second best in the controversy ; and, therefore, the reproach out of which it sprang is not the one to which I wish specially to refer. The great scandal affecting the good name of the town is at once more ancient and more serious.

The people of Thurso, according to popular tradition, are accused of having on one occasion boiled a Bishop, sometimes it is even said, *their* Bishop. This, if true, must be admitted to have been a horrible and sacrilegious crime. The charge is one which I must do my best to disprove and clear away before I can hope to enlist the interest or sympathies of my readers, even in the late posterity of such people. Let me at once begin with the frank and honest admission that within a few miles of Thurso not one but two Bishops on separate occasions came to a sad end. So much we concede freely, because we cannot do otherwise. I shall, however, show, easily and conclusively, that the people of the good town were not, in either case, the criminal parties. A simple recital of facts will show how baseless is the charge, and I shall therefore narrate the two events as they occurred.

The first case dates back so far as the latter years of the twelfth century. At that time Harold, Earl of Orkney, was ruler over all Caithness, but King William the Lion requested and commissioned Reginald, sometimes called Rognvald, Lord of the Isles, to bring back the county to its allegiance by force of arms. The royalist expedition was, after a sore struggle, successful; and Reginald on departing left deputies to rule over Caithness in the King's name. During that campaign Thurso had espoused the cause of the crown. Very soon after, Harold, who well deserved the name of the " wicked Earl Harold," returned to Caithness with a strong force of Orkneymen and Norwegians, for the purpose of re-establishing over the county his own authority and rule. He landed at Scrabster, so that Thurso was naturally his first object of attack. The townspeople, in great alarm, applied to Bishop John, whose palace lay between the town and the invading army, to intercede on their behalf. The Bishop, espousing their cause, met the Earl face to face, and earnestly pled with him to extend mercy to the inhabitants. Harold was not a man at all likely to be moved by such an appeal. Instead of appeasing, it inflamed his wrath, and the Bishop himself was made its first victim. The Earl, without a word of reply, ordered one of his followers, named Lomberd, to seize the prelate, cut out his tongue, and tear out both his eyes. The foul, dastardly deed was done, and the Bishop fell a martyr to his advocacy of the people's cause. Immediately after, the Earl wreaked his vengeance on the town itself, and hung many of its chief inhabitants. Lomberd, who so cruelly killed the Bishop, was afterwards condemned by the Pope to undergo a frightful penance, but the Earl himself—the more's the pity !—was never taken to task, and was at a later date actually forgiven by the King. In this instance at least it is clear that the people of Thurso were in no way responsible for the cruel murder of the Bishop, though their sad plight led to the commission of the crime.

In the second case, the inhabitants of Thurso, as such, were equally guiltless, though it is just possible that one or two natives of the town may have known too much of the crime. I shall even go the length of saying, that many of the Thurso people may have cried, " Served him right," when they heard of the victim's fate. The story is as follows. In the year 1222, Adam, Bishop of Caithness, occupied the Episcopal palace, which stood by the river of Thurso, five or six miles from the town. On the opposite bank of the stream, and crowning a picturesque rock, rose the strong and stately walls of the Castle of Brawl, originally spelt Brathwell, the residence at that time of John, Earl of Caithness. The Bishop was a rigid exactor of tithe, and, at short intervals, increased more and more his demands upon the people. Among other things, he required of each family a certain quantity of butter, first from every fifteen cows, then, without abatement, from every twelve cows, and, finally, from every ten cows. As the demand, even in its original form, was sufficiently heavy and galling, this growing imposition exasperated the people, who appealed their case to the Earl at Brawl. At first he declined to interfere, or even to express any opinion ; but at length he gave way to their urgent representations. Caring little for the Bishop or his claims, and worried by the clamour of the people, he testily exclaimed, "Devil take the Bishop and his butter ; you may roast him if you please." According to another version, the latter portion of his words was even less elegant than the above, namely, "Go and seethe him, and sup him, too, if you like." The crowd understood the Earl's vigorous language as a *carte blanche* permission to treat the Bishop as they pleased, and they acted accordingly. Proceeding to the palace across the river, and with cries of "Roast him alive," the mob surrounded the building. When a monk named Serlo came out to appease their rage, they attacked and despatched him on the spot. Next, the Sheriff of the county attempted to pacify them, but in vain. At length, the Bishop himself, in full sacerdotal costume, appeared, and on him their full fury burst. They seized him, and, according to one account, dragged him along by the hair, and beat him with sticks as they went. At length they conveyed him to his own large kitchen, where the fire had been abundantly replenished ; and there—they roasted him to death ! The chief actors in the tragedy are said to have been the family or followers of one John of Harpsdale, a township in the heights of the parish of Halkirk. Nothing can be said in defence or extenuation of so horrible an outrage, but at the same time we may, I think, draw one inference from the story. Considering the tremendous power of the Romish Church at that period, the Bishop's conduct must, in more ways than one, have been irritating and exasperating, else no body of men would brave the consequences of such a deed to obtain deliverance from his tyranny. Still let us trust he was a good man after all. It has been said that everything suffers by translation except a Bishop. If that adage always holds true, we may hope that Bishop Adam did not suffer by *his* translation, though the manner of it was quite unique. So far as I am aware, no Bishop has ever resided in Caithness since these days ; and it may be well for any such, who *must* pass through the county, to make their stay as brief and unostentatious as possible. Some lingering drops of the old blood may even yet remain in the veins of the people. So it has often happened among the tribes and nations of men, for there is much truth in the doctrine of heredity. Has not the poet said,

> " Thus fought the Greek of old,
>   Thus will he fight again ;
> Shall not the self-same mould
>   Bring forth the self-same men ? "

It is surely not too much to hope that my readers do not

now heed the cruel reproach against the people of Thurso.
Much rather would I believe, or allow others to believe,
in their drowsy propensities during divine service. As-
suming, however, that all prejudice is removed, allow me
now to offer some sketches, written and otherwise, of
certain inhabitants of the town.

In Thurso, as in many similar communities, there
existed what is commonly called a Dame's School,
which was maintained by public subscription. It met
in humble, and by no means extensive, premises, and
was attended by a fair number of the lasses of the town.
The mistress was a vigorous, but somewhat eccentric,
female, considerably past middle life. The ladies of the
town took an active and practical interest in the little
school, and frequently honoured it with a visit. On these
great occasions, the mistress was in full feather, and put
the frightened girls through their facings in grand style.
The programme of proceedings usually began in the
following remarkable and quite original fashion. The
ladies were accommodated with seats on either hand of
the teacher, while the girls, meek even to demureness,
filled a front bench in the middle. Addressing the
ladies, the mistress began by assuring them that her
class was composed of the stupidest, laziest, most ill-man-
nered, and ill-behaved pupils she had ever known or
even heard of. With a wealth and variety of language
which I cannot emulate, she appeared to show conclusively what a ne'er-do-weel lot they were. Having
thus unburdened her soul, and prepared the ladies to expect no trace of any excellence whatever, she turned to

the trembling young creatures whom she had so abused, and, in an encouraging tone, exclaimed,

"Noo, lasses, stan' up an' mak' yir mistress a leear."

The girls rose at once in response to this call and did their best, at the command of their teacher, to show that she really deserved the odious character which she desired to have fastened upon her. This was the invariable introduction to the work of examination, which then proceeded with all briskness. How far it would prove successful in a modern Board School and before a Government inspector, I leave to the Educational Institute of Scotland to decide. If they choose to recommend the plan to teachers generally, it might lead to interesting results.

It is now time to introduce to my readers three famous "characters," whose faces, figures, and frailties were well known in Thurso fifty years ago or more. As I am happily, or unhappily, too young to have seen any of them, my information regarding them is derived entirely from hearsay and may not be, in all points and absolutely, true to fact. At the same time I have endeavoured to do them no injustice whatever. Fortunately I am saved the trouble of attempting to describe their persons. The graphic pictures of each of the three worthies which adorn and enliven this chapter convey to the eye a faithful representation of what manner of men they were. The sketches from which these are taken were executed by a Thurso lady, a relative of my own, but were not secured without some difficulty. One at least of the gentlemen was as strongly opposed to any pictorial re-

presentation of his face and figure as any faithful Maho-
metan could possibly be, but I have reason to believe
that a little pardonable bribery overcame his scruples.
In each case the kitchen of Shrubbery Bank, Thurso,
became the studio, and there the works were executed.

We shall begin with "Peelans," or "Pillans," whose
lively likeness you will find on the opposite page. His
proper name is said to have been John M'Lean. He
was, however, universally known by the nickname, that
is, *eke-name*, which I have given above, but the origin
or meaning of which I am quite unable to explain. He
does not appear to have been a native of Thurso, and is
said to have come from the West Highlands. The
M'Lean country lay in the district of Morven and
neighbouring island of Mull.

In the case of "Peelans," we have a traditional story
as to the origin of his mental aberration. It is gruesome
enough in all conscience. When quite a young boy he
had been guilty of some petty theft. His father, to
mark his righteous indignation, devised a most remarkable and reprehensible punishment. He filled a fish
creel with a large number of frogs, well knowing that
his son had a special abhorrence of these loathsome
creatures. Into that creel, along with the frogs, he
deposited his guilty son, and then deliberately set it on
a lively fire. What the father intended the issue of that
proceeding to be, we cannot say; but Peelans in some
way or other escaped the sad fate of Bishop Adam.
From that very hour, indignant and enraged, he quitted
his father's roof never to return. The incident quite

unhinged his mind, and he became the strange, witless creature he ever after was.

No one who looks at his grotesque figure will wonder that his gait and attitudes were very peculiar. In his later days he often attracted attention by the oddity of his motions. In walking, he frequently came to an abrupt halt as if arrested by the sudden remembrance of something he had forgotten; he then stood for a few moments stock still with his feet widely apart, while his body bobbed up and down, up and down, in a jerking fashion, as if moved by some automatic mechanism.

Like many of his class, he often gave way to sullen and sulky fits. These were often produced by the unthinking, if not unkind, treatment which he received from pitiless neighbours. On one occasion he had been rudely handled by a herd boy. By way of revenge, which, unfortunately, could not affect the offender, he sat down bodily in a pool of filthy water, from which, for a length of time, no entreaties could induce him to arise. By-and-bye, a kindly Christian woman, taking pity upon him, lifted him up, and actually carried him off on her back. It is to be hoped that this benevolent action drew him out of his sulks.

At times his sullenness grew into positive and vindictive rage. His chief tormentors were boys, who delighted to annoy him in every possible way. The youth of the towns were most frequently the offenders, and sometimes, because of them, Peelans avoided Wick and Thurso for weeks and even months at a time. In dealing with his juvenile enemies, he used one peculiar

formula on almost all occasions. In scornful tones he
hurled at them the oft-needed advice, "Go to school,
Johnnie, boy." When stung into fury, he made powerful
and effective use of a sturdy stick which he always
carried as a weapon of defence. Those who had once
felt its force seldom did anything which might provoke
a second blow. On one occasion he appears to have
used it, without any due provocation, in a wantonly
wicked and cruel fashion. At a country fair, he came
in contact with a woman named Elizabeth, whom he
struck so violently, as to leave her wounded and
bleeding. No one seems to have known the cause of this
assault. A number of men gathered around and upbraided
him for his cruel and cowardly act. In a fawning,
mock-humble fashion, Peclans could only plead, "Och!
wha is't but 'dulskey Leezag'?" The latter word was
a familiar form of Elizabeth, and the "dulskey" was an
allusion to her avocation. She went about the country
selling dulse, a sea-plant of not unpleasant edible
properties. Thus Peclans expressed his contempt for the
woman, perhaps because of her sex, perhaps because of
her humble occupation, perhaps because of both.

Failing his trusty stick, anything came handy to him
for purposes of aggression. In days when newspapers
were less common than they now are, two neighbours
had a certain journal which passed regularly between
them. A youth asked permission to go for the paper to
one of the houses. He knew that Peclans was there,
and probably sought to get some fun out of him. He
found his intended victim lying on a "shake-down"

before the fire behind the "hallan" or "hallan stane" which sheltered the hearth from the draft of the door. On the entrance of the boy, Peelans at once suspected that he had to do with one of his traditional enemies, and slily took the initiative in hostilities. Rising from his resting-place, and stooping down under pretence of putting on some article of clothing, he lifted a large "tusker" peat of the hardest material, and, with the usual exclamation, " Go to school, Johnnie, boy," hurled it at the lad's head. Fortunately he missed his aim, and the peat striking the opposite wall broke into a wide-spreading cloud of dust. The good woman of the house was horrified, but not a little thankful that the missile had not reached its intended victim.

Notwithstanding these unfavourable traits in his character, Peelans appears to have had some good inclinations in the direction of religion. Many pious people thought him nearer to the kingdom than others who made sport of his mental infirmity. Peelans carried no purse nor scrip, but these good folks treated him kindly, and generously supplied his wants. He never sat down to any food provided for him without devoutly saying his " grace before meat." The wording of this devotional exercise was most remarkable and mysterious. One who has frequently heard it has kindly supplied me with the following phonetic rendering : " Los mas boce, jeca ; ooas, God ambean ; Los mas boce, jeca." When very hungry, and anxious to attack the viands before him, he used the shortened form, " Los mas boce, jeea ; ooas God ambean." If any of my readers can interpret these words, I shall be glad to be furnished with a translation. I hope I shall offend no one by suggesting that they look like Gaelic. On other occasions, Peelans used a short but intelligible prayer, which ran thus: "God made me, an' God save me—a poor ketar," that is, creature. Surely these words resemble the brief petition of the publican, "God be merciful to me the sinner." Let us hope they were uttered in a like spirit, and with a like result.

Peelans lived in the days of the first Napoleon, when volunteering was the order of the day all over Britain, even in the far north. Many of the landed proprietors and wealthier farmers took a lead in the movement. They and their sons became officers in the various companies. The drilling of recruits went on actively all over the county; and whenever Peelans could be present on such occasions, he was a deeply interested spectator. Martial dress and music had a peculiar fascination for him, and at times his enthusiasm knew no bounds. Most faithfully did he endeavour to imitate their various motions, and his attempts awakened no little hilarity among both officers and men.

Of all the military exercises, the practice of shooting interested him most, and his delight at times amounted almost to frenzy. On one occasion Peelans was on the drill field, and at a critical moment shouted out, "Present —cock—fire!" The men in the ranks mistook his voice for that of their Captain, and at once obeyed the command. They soon discovered how and by whom they had been deceived. Whether they were taken upon

M

discipline for this breach of order we are not informed. One thing is certain ; they were known for many a long day as " Peelans' squad." It is also said that in drinking bouts, the reproach of that name often led to high words, and sometimes even to bloodshed.

By those who knew his military ardour, Peelans was often asked to " call the roll." It afforded a trick which was sometimes played off on those who were not aware in what fashion he performed the duty. When the centre of a little company, some one would suggest, " Peelans, call the roll." The would-be officer at once responded, and his *modus operandi* was as follows :— He began by lifting his stick and bringing it down vigorously on the head or any other accessible part of the unfortunate individual nearest to him. This was an authoritative beginning, and afforded no little merriment to all except the poor victim. He then proceeded to call over a list of what sounded like names, but no one could ever make anything of them. If the confused syllables represented any persons whatever, no one could ever discover who they were. They might certainly absent themselves from the muster and have no fear of being called to account. Another strange character in Thurso was one Davie Rugg. Sometimes he and Peelans met in the same house. When this occurred, Rugg was in the habit of saying to the master or mistress, " Gie 'im a piece ; Lord help 'im ; he's a feel," that is, a fool. Many who knew them both were of opinion that Davie was himself the bigger fool of the two. As I have heard little of Rugg, I have no means of judging between them.

Another of the notable characters of Thurso was "Moozie," or more fully, "Johnnie Moozie," whose portrait faces this page. His real name was John Henderson, but he had quite a number of nicknames, such as "Glossey," "Starney," "Buckteeth," and "Rotten Legs." He was a married man, but little is now known of his family history. He was called "Moozie" from a cause which it would not be for edification to mention. The sketch given is a faithful reproduction of his personal appearance. Every one can see at a glance how odd was his figure and how comical his costume. Moozie had a multiplicity of offices and occupations. He was church-officer and bellman, gravedigger, town crier, officer of court, door-keeper at public meetings and entertainments, confidential messenger on all sorts of errands, and a "generally useful" person in many other ways.

Moozie was certainly most eccentric in character, but he was no fool in the ordinary acceptation of that term. He was shrewd and witty, and if his blunders were often comical, they were not due so much to any deficiency of intellect as to simple want of thought. In many cases his errors arose from the fact that he had never received a sound education.

One characteristic, not usually to be found in those of weak mind, was his strict fidelity and honesty. Because of this merit, he was often employed on errands of trust. One of the Thurso bankers at times sent him all the way to Inverness with considerable sums of money. Here are some of Moozie's reminiscences, given, I believe, very nearly in his own language, of two of these journeys. The first story is very brief—

"I hed often to go wi' money from the bank til Inverness, an' I traivelled on foot all the wey. Ae time, when sittin' on a hillag atin' something, Davie Marshall (a noted robber) cam' til me an' said, 'Ye hev money in 'at bag.' I said, "Yes," 'an I laid doon ma pistals aside it. I wis feared he micht tak' 'e money, but he gaed awa withoot touchin't."

The next is a longer story.

"Ae time Maister Henderson (the banker) sent for me. I wis livin' then at Thirsay (Thurso) east. He said til me, 'John, you must go to Inverness with money to-day. Get ready as quick as ye can and mind to go with daylight and take up your lodgings when night comes on.' I wis busy wi' some wark at hame so I wis in nae hurry startin'. He ca'ed at 'e hoose an' wis vera angry for me stoppin' sae lang. I got 'e wallat frae 'im wi' 'e money. There wis fine snaw an' frost at 'e time an' bonnie mune licht. I sterted in 'e efterneen an' when I cam til Achkeepster Inn I thocht at first I wud pit up 'ere. Bit when I lookit oot an' saw 'e nicht sae clear, I says til masel, 'Gad, I'll go on.' When I cam til 'e burn o' Rangag, I laid doon ma wallat an' boo'ed doon til tak' a drink. I notticed twa men on 'e aff side —ane on horseback an' 'e ither on feet. I cried 'Wha's ere?' but nae answer. I cries a second time, 'Wha's 'ere?'—still nae answer. I taks oot ane o' ma pistals an' fires her. They said, 'Man, are ye mad?' 'Na,' says I, 'I'm nae mad, bit *ye're* mad. Whey wadna ye

answer a buddy whan he cried? This ane brunt primin,
but, faith, gin I hed ta'en 'e ither, she wadna miss'd.'
Whan they cam' across 'e watter I saw 'at 'it wis a
gaeger an' 'e superveesor. They hed been aff scoorin' 'e
country in search o' smugglers. I didna ken bit they
micht be robbers an' as I wis trusted wi' 'e money I wad
hae a fecht afore I wad lose it."

As an evidence of his employment as door-keeper at
entertainments, it may be sufficient to quote the following quaint couplet referring to some such occasion,

> "There was a ball in Murray's hall, got up by Snuffy Diddle ;
> Ringie Moozie kept the door, an' Sooky Almon' played the fiddle."

Moozie of course was called "Ringie" because of his
office as bellman. As to the other elegant personal allu-
sions in the lines, it is perhaps as well that I cannot
explain them. Still, it is possible that even at this time
of day they may be understood by some local parties.

As already mentioned, "Buckteeth" was one of
Moozie's nicknames. It was evidently an allusion to his
prominent and even protruding front teeth. Johnnie
did not like the epithet and frequently resented its
application. On one occasion, while standing in a
grocer's shop in Thurso, a woman said to him, "Johnnie,
why do they ca' ye Buckteeth? Ye hae as bonnie
teeth as ither folk." Moozie's cunning answer was,
"Wumman, I hae something mair extrordnar than 'at.
I hae hair growin' in ma mooth, 'an if ye pit yer finger in,
ye'll feel't." The silly woman did as she was bidden.
Moozie bit her finger almost to the bone, and then said
with a satisfied grin, "Gad, 'at 'ill learn ye no til ca' me

Buckteeth again." Most likely she profited by the lesson.

In Johnnie Moozie's days, the "cutty stool" was still used in church as a means of punishment for those guilty of offences against chastity. It was his duty to arrange the sackcloth and stool on such occasions, and he was always strict and often severe in the discharge of his functions. In one instance a woman was the unfortunate offender with whom he had to deal, and she proved rather refractory. Johnnie set her up to stand on the stool but while he was occupied with some detail of the ceremony, she slipped down and stood upon the floor. Again he ordered her to mount the place of penitence, and again, when his back was turned, she descended from the perch of shame. This contumacy fairly roused Moozie's anger, and in a voice which was heard by most of those present in church, he thundered out the command,

"Get up, ye ——, an' stan' on't, an' if ye dinna stan', I'll bin' (bind) ye on't, for weel dis yir sins deserv't."

If Moozie lived in our day, I am not sorry to say that as regards these duties he would find his occupation gone, like many another relic of barbarism.

At times Moozie came off second best in his dealings with offenders. It seems there was a sort of lock-up in Thurso for mischievous boys, and Johnnie was the warder. He rather enjoyed the process and privilege of shutting up these juvenile criminals under lock and key in that chamber of durance vile. One day, however, the boys turned the tables on him; they were literally *too many* for their gaoler. When he entered to give them some food, they fell upon him in a body, bound him with ropes, and laid him groaning and moaning upon the floor. To make all secure, they locked the door behind them and made their escape with all possible speed. At length Moozie's shouts for help were heard, and after some time and trouble he was released from bondage.

It has been mentioned that Moozie was sexton of the parish. In this capacity it does not appear that he gave entire satisfaction. On one occasion a poor widow complained to the minister—the Rev. Mr Macintosh—that she had been overcharged for the expenses of her husband's funeral. The amount demanded by Johnnie was seven shillings and sixpence. When the minister stated the widow's complaint, and asked for an explanation, Moozie was indignant, and by way of self-defence asked Mr Macintosh some questions. "Did she tell ye 'at 'e grave was dug six feet instead o' five?" "No, John," said the minister, "she did not." "Did she tell ye she had 'e eess (use) o' 'e murt-cloth?"—a black pall thrown over the coffin. The minister had again to confess she had not. "'Ats 'e wey, Maister Macintosh, 'e d—— set 'ill come til ye wi' their blue cloaks an' white mutches. Ye'll gie them tea an' a' 'e rest o't, an' they'll tell ye a lot o' d—— lees." The minister rebuked him for his profane language, but Moozie evidently could not control himself, for he replied, "Gad, it wad mak' a sa'nt sweer. 'E grave wis dug six feet instead o' five — that's sax shillins; an' 'e cess o' 'e murt-cloth wis eichteen pence."

Apparently there was no reply to that statement of the account.

At certain seasons Moozie wrought along with others in the field work of the manse glebe. Toward the close of a day's work, the minister came with a bottle of whisky and gave a glass to each of the men. When all these had been supplied, Johnnie asked the Rev. gentleman, " Are ye no til gie a dram til 'e weemen ? " " No," said the minister, " the women don't drink." Johnnie met this statement by way of analogy. " Is 'at what ye say ? Eh, 'e dukes 'ill drink as weel's 'e drakes." Probably the minister did not consider that style of argument sufficient in such a case.

Moozie, being bellman of the Kirk, was also town crier. Let me give a specimen or two of the manner in which he discharged that important public function. In one case he was commissioned to make the following announcement by hand-bell throughout the town: "Mr —— of — will deliver a Lecture this evening on Geography and Biography." Moozie proceeded to discharge his duty, and at every customary corner in the streets rung his bell vigorously, and proclaimed aloud, " Mr — — of — will deliver a Lecture this evening on Gography and Bography." At another time, some one, as a practical joke, paid him his usual fee of sixpence, and sent him out with the following notice : " Lost, last night, an empty pock fu' o' sawt (salt). Any person bringing the said pock to me will be liberally rewarded for their trouble." At one point in his journey, a passer-by remonstrated with him as to the nature of his announcement. "Johnnie, what nonsense is that? How can the pock be empty and full of salt?" Moozie at once replied, "Weel, I noor (never) thocht o' 'at; but deil cares, I hae 'e saxpence." He probably went on his way to accomplish the usual round.

Probably Moozie's most important office—next, at least, to that of bellman—was officer of court. His discharge of the duties, however, was often marked by eccentricities and blunders. In one particular case—I cannot tell its nature—a man, whose name was Sullivan Keith, was required to appear in Court. The names were apparently unfamiliar to Johnnie, but, of course, he would on no account confess ignorance, or even seem to be beaten. As he must needs cry out some names, he hit upon a happy paraphrase, and with dignity exclaimed, "Silver Teeth, to answer at the instance of so and so. Silver Teeth, once; Silver Teeth, twice; Silver Teeth, thrice. He's not in the house, my Lord."

I have one more incident in the life of Moozie to record. In these days the punishments inflicted on thieves and other criminals were often remarkable. Sometimes they were condemned to be "tied to a cart's tail," and flogged through the streets of the town. In a certain case of the class mentioned, this peculiar sentence was pronounced, and then the presiding Justices had to face the question who should be deputed to do the flogging. The Laird of Freswick, who was a Sinclair, and who delighted to recount Moozie's many titles, said, "Moozie will whip him." One of the other justices who knew, or pretended to know, very little of Johnnie, at once asked, "Who is that?" By way of mischief and fun, Freswick varied the name. "Glossey will whip him." Still the justices professed ignorance of the individual proposed, so Sinclair gave them a still further choice of the names of his nominee, "Starney, Buckteeth, Rotten Legs, Johnnie Henderson, Moozie will do it." By this time there was no possibility of mistake. Johnnie, who was present all the while, was at length asked if he would consent to perform the official duty, but, being indignant with the liberties taken with his name, at once replied, "Na, na, I'll no feep (whip) 'im. The Sinclairs hae hed 'a 'e honours in Caitness 'is mony a day, 'an 'ey can tak' 'at wi' 'e lave." This biting retort upon the Laird of Freswick caused no little amusement, and as a reward, a gentleman named Henderson gave Moozie a sovereign to drink his health. Johnnie would no doubt receive the gift with thankfulness. Who was ultimately induced to execute the sentence, I do not know. It may be safely taken for granted, however, that the Laird of Freswick, like Moozie himself, would decline the honour.

The third and most original of all the Thurso "characters" was Neil Mackay, whose by-name was "Boustie." He does not appear to have been a native of the town; perhaps he came from the Reay country, the home and territory of the clan whose name he bore. Why he was called "Boustie," it is impossible to affirm with any certainty. The most probable suggestion is that the name was originally "Boastie," and was intended to describe his braggart character. He had several other

nicknames, such as " Bushans," " Bushey Neilic," and " Mally sookit 'e coo." The last of these was, I fear, the property, strictly speaking, of his wife, but was on a well-known principle of matrimony applied also to the husband.

As to his personal appearance, I refer my readers to his portrait, for which he consented to sit, or rather stand, after much persuasion both in the shape of argument and money. His figure was erect and not wanting in a certain rude dignity. His nose was decidedly prominent, and his under-lip often hung down like the mouth of a cream jug. His eyeballs rolled about restlessly and were raised upward beneath their caves when narrating his biggest fibs, as if appealing to high heaven for their truthfulness.

As has already been said, no one knows whence or when he came to Caithness, though the general belief is that he was a native of the West Highlands. According to common tradition, he was first seen in the neighbourhood of Holborn Head, but how, whence, or why he came thither, is an insoluble mystery. One story is that he fell down from the sky like a meteor, but no one could ever find anything about his person or character to support any such view. If an angel, he was certainly a fallen one. He had without doubt not a little affinity of moral sentiment with the father of lies. According to another account, he came to the Caithness coast on an emigrant vessel, from which he somehow made his escape either of his own accord, or when she was wrecked. Yet another tradition is that he spent part of his early life as a mason's labourer in Edinburgh. It is further supposed that he there acquired those aristocratic airs which often astonished the simple townspeople of Thurso, and even tickled the fancy of his more cultured and high caste acquaintances.

One of Boustie's most marked characteristics was his intense and peculiar pride. He believed himself to be a born aristocrat, and it was one of the motive forces of his life to maintain and act up to that high dignity. In the matter of charity, this feature always came prominently to the front. He never would accept of any gift or alms as an ordinary beggar or in an ordinary way ; in fact, he would scorn to stoop so low. But those who knew him well were aware of this peculiarity, and found out how it might be overcome to the satisfaction of all parties. If the gift were presented as the return of a loan, Boustie would willingly and with dignity consent to accept payment. Let the giver say with polite deference, " Mr Mackay, here is the sixpence I borrowed from you a week ago." Boustie would pocket it at once, very often adding the remark, " Yes, an' it's time it wis paid too." The late Mr Dunbar of Scrabster often slipped something into his hand when he thought no one was likely to notice. One day a few young men, suspecting that Boustie had got some money from his benefactor, cried to him, " Boustie— beggary! beggary ! " " Mr Mackay " at once drew himself up proudly, and replied, " Nacthing o' 'c kind ; it's a shillin' I lent 'im whan he wis buyan' fish at 'e fish-stane." At times, perhaps when he was in straits, Boustie ventured to give a hint to his wealthier friends, but the hint also ran along the familiar lines. If he saw any lady or gentleman buy something, fish or any similar article, he would stand quietly by until the bargain was completed and the money paid. Then, supposing it were a gentleman, Boustie would mutter in a gentle aside, as if addressing himself alone, " It wad set (become) him far better 'e pay me fat (what) he borrowed 'e last year." He then went on his sorrowful way to moralise upon the ingratitude and dishonesty of mankind. These little ways of showing his proud nature pleased him, and did no harm to any body.

Soon after coming to Thurso, Boustie took unto him a wife. She was a woman named Mally Forsyth, who, though good looking, was of weak intellect like himself. She died long before him, and her funeral was a remark- able occasion in his history. It is a strange comment on human nature to observe how certain persons acquire great importance in their own eyes if they are the chief actors in proceedings connected with death or burial. The prominence which they necessarily assume, the sympathy and consideration extended to them, the superior dress they wear on such occasions : all these combine to raise them in their own estimation, and to induce them to put on airs which at other times they would never think of displaying. Before alluding to this feeling as shown in his own peculiar fashion by Boustie, let me confirm what I have said by an instance from another quarter of the country. In a Scotch low-

land town there lived a woman of weak intellect who
imbibed the notion that several gentlemen were greatly
taken with her charms.   One of her supposed admirers
was a clergyman in the town, who, however, disappointed
her by marrying another.   A few years afterwards he
died.   On the occasion of his funeral, the poor creature
referred to stood among a group of spectators as the
cortege passed through the streets, and she was observed
to be weeping.   When some one asked her the cause
of her tears, she, with much apparent emotion, replied,
" If it hedna been for ma mither, I micht hae been the
widow the day."   The lot of the real widow on that
occasion was in her opinion one to be envied.

Well, something of the same strange feeling seems to
have possessed Boustie on the occasion of his wife
Mally's funeral.   Being the aristocrat he was, he was
resolved to appear to the very best advantage at so
important a public ceremony.   There were not wanting
in Thurso those who were quite disposed to humour him
to the top of his bent in such a matter.   A few of the
tailors in town resolved and offered to rig him out in
becoming fashion for the ceremony.   Little suspecting
their waggish intentions, he gratefully accepted their
services.   I am sorry I cannot fully describe the striking
costume which was the fruit of their labours, but I can
mention one or two of the articles.   Among county
gentlemen and other persons of quality, tall white felt
hats were fashionable at the time, so, to make him equal
with his peers, one of these dashing head-pieces was provided for Boustie.   They further adorned it with long,

profuse bands of crape, whose folds hung far down his back. So attired, he followed Mally's remains to the graveyard, with a solemn and haughty dignity which could not have been exceeded had he been the Earl of Caithness or the Chief of his own famous clan.

If his name was given him because he was a boaster, it was most appropriate, for this at all events is certain, that he was habitually guilty of extravagant lying and bragging. He detailed his own exploits with the utmost calmness and solemnity. They never appeared to him in the least degree improbable, unreal, or untrue. The biggest lie which his brain could invent, he told with the most innocent and guileless of all looks. As few who heard cared to question his wonderful tales, he resented the slightest sign of incredulity on the part of a listener.

As one of his minor exploits—in fact, scarcely worth mentioning—he often told how he had, without any assistance, built a bridge over the water of Forse in the darkness of a single night. Surely this, small though it be, compares well even with the labours of Hercules. The mighty deed was done as a service to his good friend, Mr Sinclair of Forse, and became necessary because of some dispute with Mr Innes, the laird of Sandside. As this was quite a trifling event, of which I have not heard all the details, we shall pass on to exploits which were obviously designed on a much more imposing scale.

One of these was a great feat, the scene of which lay on Holborn Head. We have already spoken of the

Clett, a massive stack standing out in the northern sea at a distance of perhaps 80 yards from the main wall of cliffs. Few have ever been found who could throw a stone from the rock-heads on to its summit. But the distance was nothing to Boustie. He most solemnly declared that he had once, holding a sack of meal in his teeth, leapt clean over from the headland on to the Clett and landed safely on its crown. He might there sing with Robinson Crusoe, though Juan Fernandez was somewhat larger,

> " I am monarch of all I survey,
>   My right there is none to dispute ;
> From the centre all round to the sea
>   I am lord of the fowl and the brute."

But Boustie had no intention of taking up his abode on the Clett ; he might even roll off in his sleep. The return, however, was more difficult and must be described, as nearly as may be, in his own words. " I couldna get a rinnen' leap, but whan half wey ower, I gied anither spring an' landed on Hobran Heed." Apparently some sceptical person had expressed a doubt as to whether such a feat was practicable, for Boustie sometimes explained the matter in another fashion. According to this variety of the story, our hero watched his opportunity, and when a mighty eagle was sailing across between the stack and the land, he leapt on its back, and when carried over the brow of the cliffs, dropped from his wonderful saddle safely to the ground. Such were the two accounts. If any persons were disposed to question either version, they were welcome to accept the alternative form. No one will doubt the truth of the second account who remembers a similar exploit on the part of Sinbad the Sailor, in whom we have all believed since our early days.

According to his own story, for which there is possibly a foundation in fact, Boustie had been at one time a sailor. His adventures at sea were very remarkable, especially as these were narrated by his own lips. One who knew him well has supplied me with the following story which is as nearly as possible a reproduction of his own language. I might run the risk of marring the simple truthfulness which appears upon the very surface of the account, if I were to attempt any paraphrase. Please allow me a word upon the Caithness dialect. *Th* is almost universally cut off, so that *that* becomes *'at*, *the* becomes *'e*. *Til* (which for distinction I spell with one *l*) is always used for *to*; and readers will notice a strong tendency to cut short many of the words.

Well, a certain person met Boustie one day, and after salutation said, "You're looking very well to-day, Mr Mackay; I hope you will have a long life yet." Boustie was in good humour, and very soon launched out upon his sea adventures. "Oh no, jewel, I'm a vera old man now, an' 'am sairly bathered wi' 'e rout. (I presume that means asthma, or difficulty in breathing.) I wis a sailor aince, jewel; I wis eichteen year at sea, an' three year o' 'at I nivver saw day-licht. I wis wi' Cappin Manson—as guid a sailor as ever set feet on sawt watter. Bit ae day a terrible storm cam' on, an' Cappin Manson sed til me, 'Hae, ye black souroo (devil), tak'

N

'ir (the ship) an' do wi' 'ir fat ye like for 'am dune wi'
'ir.' So I pit e' men under hatches, an' lash't masel til
'e helem. I steered 'ir intil a place 'at 'ey ca' Bell Pint.
'Ere wis a lot o' cappins o' cod-bangers on shore, an' 'ey
'a kent Cappin Manson. Ane o' 'em sed til 'im, 'Dear
me, Cappin Manson, hoo did ye mak' 'd oot. We nivver
thocht 'at ye wad mak' 'd oot.' 'E Cappin said, 'I
hev nae credit for't; it wis 'at auld black souroo 'at did
it.' Bit it wis a terrible cowld place, jewel. It wis 'at
cowld 'at ma feet wis frozen til 'e deck, an' I hed til rin
an' get bilin' watter til lowse 'em." Such were some of
Boustie's adventures on what a northern minister once
pathetically called "the wet and stormy ocean."

The Disruption of the Church of Scotland in 1843 and
the formation of the Free Church as a body without
State connection or endowment gave rise to keen excitement. Many good people hesitated for a time whether
to remain in the Established Church, or "go out," as it
was called, with the Free. Boustie was present at a
small but influential meeting in the "Auld Kirk," at
which a few gentlemen were to discuss their own duty
in the matter. Here is Boustie's account, but how far
it is absolutely true in fact and description it is now
impossible to say. He was himself a loyal adherent of
mother Church, so it is not likely that he would make
things *very* much worse than they were. On entering
the house of an acquaintance on some errand, he was
asked where he had come from. In reply he said,
"I wis at a meetin' in 'e Kirk. C—— D—— was
'ere, W—— M——, B——Street, J——G——, 'e skeel-

maister, ma friend B—— frae Sharney Hillag. Maister
D——, daccent, godly man, wis 'ere too, an' masel. 'E
question wis, whether wid we leave 'e 'Steablish'd Kirk
or stick by 'ir. Nane o' 'em spak' for a while. At last
Maister D——, daccent, godly man, brocht 'is han'
down wi' a thump on 'e table an' said, 'G—— d—— it,
what will we do bit stick by 'e 'Steablish'd Kirk. There
wis a 'Steablished Kirk afore 'e world was, and 'ere'll
be ane efter she's dune." Of course I could give the
whole of the names of which the initials are given, but
I have come as near to the personal as courtesy will
permit. To do less would spoil my story.

In his later years Boustie was greatly alarmed by the
proposal to erect gas works in Thurso. He was con-
vinced that the town would be ruined, and all the
inhabitants killed, by some dreadful explosion. Though
at that time about ninety years of age, he proved the sincerity of his fears by travelling to Wick to consult a
lawyer on the subject. His object was to obtain an
interdict against the progress of the works, but he was
not successful. He lived in Thurso for years after in
perfect safety.

We have still one other feature in Boustie's character
to notice, and must narrate a strange adventure to which
it gave rise. It must be admitted that in one direction
at least he was a notorious thief. Peats were the chief
objects of his covetous thoughts and deeds ; and his
humble dwelling was at times so full of them that it
was almost impossible to move about on the floor. Of
course he had too much self-respect to steal openly or in

broad day-light. Under cover of night however, he sallied forth with a large sack, and helped himself liberally from his neighbours' stacks. This thievish propensity led him on one occasion into a strange adventure. It was about the time when all Scotland was ringing with the murderous deeds of Burke and Hare, who slew many a victim in the West Port of Edinburgh, and disposed of their bodies to the doctors for purposes of dissection. A few young fellows in Thurso, out on the spree and ready for any lark, detected Boustic filling his sack at a peat-stack, and resolved to play a practical joke at his expense. Catching the guilty creature in the very act, they emptied the sack of its contents and packed Boustic himself inside, in spite of all his protests and resistance. As this process was going on, they audibly whispered to one another that they would carry him off to Dr Laing and get a good round sum for his carcase. Of course they fully intended their victim to hear this proposal and decision. Poor Boustic trembled all over with fright, but what could he do? Struggle as he might, he was now helpless in their hands. All this time the young men knew well that the much-esteemed doctor was that evening a guest at a fashionable party in town. Lifting upon their shoulders the sack containing their prize, they went direct to the scene of festivity, where they no doubt hoped and intended to create some sensation. On arriving, they stuck the sack up on its end against the jamb of the door, and then rung the bell. Betaking themselves to a little distance, they awaited the result with lively interest. When the servant opened, the sack, with its shivering occupant, fell inwards on the lobby floor, and Boustie, with much difficulty, wriggled his head out of the folds of the mouth. At once dreading the worst that had been threatened him, he apostrophized the doctor in frightfully profane language, "——, —— —— Lingie, ye ——, if ye pit yir han' on me it'll be the blackest job ever ye did in yir life." Recognising his own name even in its vulgarised form, the doctor, with many of the company, rushed into the lobby and at once discovered the cause of the disturbance. Boustie's sad plight was the liveliest incident of the evening's enjoyment, and—better still—it cured him of the evil habit of peat-stealing.

Poor Boustie died about the year 1849 as the result of an accident. Being struck by the shaft of a cart and crushed between the wheel and a wall, he sustained injuries from which he never recovered. He was the chief of our three "worthies," and appears to have been a favourite with everybody in Thurso.

CHAPTER VII.

THE SHETLAND ISLANDS.

A FAMILIAR story is told of a south-country minister who spent a summer holiday in Shetland, and lectured to his own people when he returned. Choosing the Islands as his theme, he selected as his text the appropriate declaration, "There shall be no night there." As regards some six weeks in summer, the words are really true to fact, for, though Shetland is not absolutely the "land of the midnight sun," it comes nearer to that description than any other spot under the British crown, at least in Europe. This is at least one reason why of late years so many travellers visit the Islands. I trust they will not be sorely offended if I tell them that they so become what the Orkney people used in disdain to call "Ferry-loupers;" that is, *leapers over the ferry* between these groups and the mainland of Scotland. To see the sun *very near* to midnight is an interesting sight, but Shetland has far greater and more permanent attractions. To those who know them I need not say that I refer to the magnificent sea-board scenery of the Islands, and the picturesque aspects of life among a people not yet spoiled by contact with the grosser

From Photo. by G. W. Wilson.

THE GRIND OF THE NAVIR, HILLSWICK.

adjuncts of civilisation. We are still at some distance
from the time when a cantilever bridge shall be thrown
over the Pentland Firth or the Roost of Sumburgh. I
know that the visitor to Shetland may have to endure
at times a very considerable tossing by the way, but
what can he expect ? We all have our ups and downs
in this life whether on land or sea, and we must just
grin and bear them. Only the other day I read the
following sentence and took a careful note of it for the
benefit of others. "There was never yet such a storm
but it was Æolian music to a healthy and innocent ear."
There you have a choice morsel of philosophy for inward
digestion at sea when you can eat nothing else. If you
are, or even desire to be thought, healthy and innocent,
then be sure you do not grumble at the Atlantic swells
which may come from the far west to pay you their
respects between Fair Isle and Sumburgh.

Lerwick, the chief, or rather the only town in Shetland, lies on the eastern side of the main island, which
is called Mainland to distinguish it from those which
are smaller. The houses are piled up the steep sides
of a deeply-curved bay, the opposite side of which is
formed by the island of Bressay. Run your eye along
the ridge at the top of the town. It seems as if some
powerful giant had brought to the edge a mighty
waggon laden with walls, roofs, windows, gables, doors,
and chimneys, and had tilted them all over to tumble
down the slope and find a resting-place anywhere from the
crown of the height to the shelving shore. Many of the
houses stand up to their knees in the water, as if they

had come down to the beach to cool their feet and did not mean to return. Their walls are so stained as to mark plainly the level of high water, at which time a native may dive into the sea, or step into his boat, from a back door or window.

The one main street twists in and out round the sweep of the bay with thin blocks of shops and houses between it and the sea, and, on the opposite side, steep lanes which clamber up to the ridge above. This is of course the great thoroughfare and business mart of the town. The street is paved with flagstones; and is in many parts very narrow and tortuous. The reason is not far to seek. Owners and builders have stuck walls and gables at every conceivable angle one to another, and just as far out into the street as seemed good in their own eyes. The result is picturesque but awkward. If you make up your mind to walk forward in the twilight ten or twelve yards in a straight line, the chances are you will either smash your face against a gable or topple through a shop window. In this main street you may meet, in strange medley, Dutch sailors, whaling crews from Dundee, fishermen and crofters from all the isles, women bearing heavy keysies (creels) of peats and knitting as they go, ragged Shetland ponies, and jolly tourists in every freak of humour and costume. Here, also, you may note on the faces of the people the plain tokens of their Norse descent, for their Scandinavian blood is purer than that of the people of Caithness or even Orkney. These are the true-blue sons of the Vikings, who can sing of their ancestors—

"Ho ! We were a band of rovers,
  Sailing here and sailing there ;
Sailing where the wild winds bore us,
  None to stay our course might dare !

Gaily blew and roared the breezes,
  Waved our ravens on the gale !
Forward bounded Norway's galleys
  Winged with many a bellying sail."

Being the pure Norseman he is, the real Shetlander does not consider himself a Scotchman. When I first took lodgings in one of the islands, I was advised to visit a farmer, a Mr Grant, some two miles away, because, said they, "He's a Scotchman, like yourself." As, however, the islands have belonged to Scotland for not a few centuries the Shetland dialect is Scotch, with the admixture of many Norse words. You may hear its peculiar half-lisped, Quaker-like tones and forms at any corner in the main street of Lerwick.

Before launching out among the islands, I select two incidents from my memories of the chief town. On the evening of my first Sunday in Shetland, I was lodged along with a friend in the house of a respectable merchant, who did a humble trade in the town. At a somewhat late hour our landlord came into our room and sat down between us at the fireside. He had come to enjoy a chat, or, as we say in Scotland, a "crack." He was a strong man on the side of religion, and our conversation took that direction. At length—I forget how—we came to speak of the patriarch Job and his troubles, and to discuss whether his wife had been a good, pious woman or no. After some arguments, *pro* and *con*, had been advanced, the conversation took the following turn, and the turn soon led to its termination.

"Well," said our host, "I have long had a strong opinion upon that point."

"Come along, then, Mr H——," said one of us; "we have been having our say; we shall be glad to hear your view."

"Well," replied he, abruptly, "I believe she was out and out a bad woman."

"That is decided enough in all conscience," said the former speaker; "but we should like to hear your reasons. They ought to be strong to support so sweeping a charge against the old lady."

We were prepared to listen to a chain of argument made up of various particulars, but our host's logic was as concise as it was clinching. As nearly as I can remember, his words were—

"God permitted Satan to take all his good things from Job, and if his wife had been good she would have been taken too. If his wife, being a good woman, had been left to comfort him, his trial would not have been complete."

No theologian, it seems to me, could have put the matter more conclusively; and few will wonder that our after conversation took a new direction.

Some years later, during a brief visit to Shetland, I heard of a misfortune which had befallen an old friend. He was a skipper belonging to one of the northern isles, and every inch a sailor. Most vividly can I see at this moment his round, ruddy face, and hear the rapid rattle of

his cheery voice. Just before the time I speak of he had
been master of a splendid sloop—once a gentleman's yacht
—which we shall call the *Evangeline.* With her he had
been trading between Shetland and the Faroe Islands.
Magnus had a keen eye to business and profit, and was
said to have netted more than once a fair sum by smuggling. Made rash by impunity, he ventured on larger
risks, and at last came to grief. He had left the Faroe
Isles with an ordinary cargo of fish, to which he had
added several kegs of brandy and a considerable quantity
of tobacco. His intention was to land these important
extras in a quiet voe (*i.e.*, sea-loch) on the north-west of
the Mainland, and then proceed to Lerwick with his
proper cargo. The plan miscarried, like many others of
the " best laid schemes of mice and men." He had
crept into a quiet bay, and had no sooner dropped anchor
for the night than great folds of mist enveloped them.
Gliding down from Rona's (Ronald's) Hill, they wrapt
the *Evangeline* round and round. Early next morning
Magnus and his crew crawled slowly out to seaward,
hoping to get clear of the land-born fogs. In this aim
they succeeded, but, alas! it was to their intense chagrin
and serious loss. As soon as they could see a mile or
little more, there lay a revenue cutter with her raking
masts and big white sails at no great distance off. In a
moment puff came the powder-smoke from her side, and
a ball shot whirring across the bows of the sloop.
Magnus and his men, maddened and vexed, did their
very utmost, crowding all the sail they could upon the
Evangeline, but in the light fitful wind which came

through the mist they had no chance. Soon their only concern was to sink the evidences of their guilt out of sight. Creeping almost on their knees, they rolled the kegs of brandy to the gangway on the further side from the cutter, and dropped them as gently as possible into the sea. Package after package of tobacco went the same way; but a considerable quantity still remained when the cutter came alongside and the officers boarded the sloop. Magnus and his crew were at once arrested, and soon after tried at Lerwick. The skipper was sentenced to a term of imprisonment, and was confined in Fort Charlotte.

Having obtained permission, I visited him in his cell, and heard from his own lips—in true sailor lingo and with ample details—the story of his capture. I ventured to suggest how foolish and dangerous it was—to use no stronger terms—to break the Queen's laws and defy the officers of the Crown. To this view of things he made no reply. At length, however, he "turned his sad soul into smiling," for, just as I was about to leave, he brought down his fist briskly upon some invisible object, and with mingled pride and anger exclaimed: " Say what you like, if I had only had a bit of a breeze, I would soon have let them see my stern." I fear Magnus was incorrigible, and perhaps even suspected I should myself have enjoyed such a flight and chase.

If you ask me whether or no there is any smuggling still going on among these islands, I shall give as suggestive a reply as I dare. The tobacco used by the Shetlanders generally is of one well-known variety, which you will *not* see exposed in shop windows, but which I think I could get you almost anywhere without much trouble. Moreover, I should not advise a tobacconist to go and settle in Shetland ; his occupation is not needed. I remember well how on one occasion a most excellent man gave me a cake or two of first-rate tobacco. When I discourteously and foolishly asked him where he had got it, he flung the authority of St Paul at my head by saying with a peculiar smile, " Eat that which is set before thee—asking no questions for conscience' sake." I accepted the rebuke meekly, and ate, or rather smoked, with much satisfaction.

The Shetland Islands are an archipelago lying more than 100 miles north-east of Caithness, and separated even from the Orkneys by some 50 miles of open sea. The chief isles of the group are four—Mainland, Yell, Unst, and Fetlar—the first of these being about 60 miles long, the other three less than a third of that size. In addition, there are about a hundred more, which diminish gradually from those of fair dimensions like Bressay, Whalsey, and Muckle Rooe (pronounced Roo) to small holms and islets, many of which are both tenantless and nameless. The group as a whole is most irregular and ragged in contour, as if winds and waves had conspired to tear it into shreds and tatters, so that there is not a spot in Shetland three miles from the sea. Inland, the islands are bare and bleak in the extreme, and their stony or mossy undulations seldom rise even to the rank of hills ; but the coast scenery, especially in the north and west, far surpasses anything of the kind elsewhere

in the United Kingdom.   If I should attempt to describe
with any measure of fulness the cloudy cliffs of Foula,
1300 feet high ; the marble pillars and deep-sounding
caves of Papa Stour ; the fantastic freaks of nature
along the coast of Hillswick ; the countless groups of
stacks and arches and tunnels which belong to this
island or to that, I should swell out this chapter far
beyond its intended limits.   Therefore I ask you to
visit with me two districts only of widely diverse
character—the one taking its name from Yell, the other
at Hillswick on the extreme north-west of Mainland.

　　We shall first visit the Sound of Yell, which runs for
nearly 20 miles between that island and the Mainland.
More than once have I stood upon the hill-top of Clothan
in Yell, and feasted my eyes upon the immense and
varied panorama of earth and sea which is visible from
that elevated spot.   Looking first westward and then to
the south, the entire length of the Sound lies immediately before us.   The outline of its shores is most
irregular, for they often approach each other in capes,
and as often recede from one another into half-hidden
bays.   To use a homely simile, the shape of the Sound
is that of a high boot, of which the top is to the north,
the heel to the south, and the toe pointing out to the
east.   You must, however, remember that the main
colour is blue, dotted here and there with patches of
brilliant green, and these again girt round about with a
ragged fringe of brown rock and white foam.   From
this hill-top the eye may range over three quarters of
the compass—from north to west, and west to south, and

south to east; and the view embraces half the islands
of the entire group and every feature of its scenery.
Right over against us is the Mainland, dark and hilly,
with alternate cape and sea-loch (*voe* in Shetland), as if
earth and ocean had interlaced their fingers in a firm
and friendly clasp. Twelve miles away, in the north-
west, is the further extremity of the chief island, ter-
minating in savage splintered cliffs which frown upon
the sea. Still further out, a group of giant stacks, like
brown icebergs cut adrift, struggles far to seaward.
Neptune has wedged his way between and cut them off
from the shore. In time of storm they become his play-
things. The western waves creep quivering up their
precipitous sides, fall in weighty masses on their heads,
and then sink down in cataracts of foam, like the white
tresses on an old man's shoulders.

All up and down the course of the Sound lie islands
and clusters of islets like green leaves, some of them
tinged with grey or brown, floating down the broad
current. Between these the tides rush and roar incessantly, and in many places dash along at the rate of ten
miles an hour. Sometimes they form wide whirling
curves, with tiny white threads of foam upon their edges;
at other times they leap and dance like thousands of
pointed flames, and then woe betide the silly boat which
ventures among them! How the natives laugh and jeer
when they see a whaling steamer attempting to pass up
the Sound against the flood-tide! Well do they know
that engines and helm are alike useless, and that very soon
she will turn aside and run for some sheltered voe where

she may hide from view her failure and her shame. Away to the south lie cape and then bay, cape and then bay, as far as the bold headland of Noss, and on the eastern horizon you may see the long line of the Out Skerries, large and small, like a fleet of boats with white sails full set making for Norway "over the faem." Looking once more over the moorland ridges and hills of the Mainland, we behold, standing up against the distant sky, the stupendous precipices of Foula, not less at their loftiest point than 1300 feet high. Supreme over all their kind, they rear their iron front defiantly against the western ocean. Yet again, far overhead, as we sit on this hill-top, the kingly eagle in stately sail looks down with scorn upon the world beneath ; and from the rocks below there rise fitfully the babbling and screeching of thousands upon thousands of sea-birds, ever flitting and whirling over land and tide.

There is little in the scene before us, extensive and varied though it be, to be called sweet or beautiful as these terms are generally understood. There is not a tree to be seen within range of the eye from this spot ; no broad fruitful fields ; no gardens of flowers ; little delicate shading and softness of colour. Yet there is breadth, and strength, and grandeur ; variety to feed the mind with ever-new discoveries ; bold and cunning strokes of nature's handiwork to stimulate and inspire.

> "Here rise no groves and here no gardens blow,
> Here e'en the hardy heath scarce dares to grow ;
> But rocks on rocks, in mist and storm arrayed,
> Stretch far to sea their giant colonnade—

With many a cavern seamed, the dreary haunt
Of the dun seal and swarthy cormorant.
Wild round their rifted brows with frequent cry
As of lament, the gulls and gannets fly,
And from their sable base, with sullen sound,
In sheets of whitening foam the waves rebound."

The sea—the wild, the glorious sea—is the dominant power over all. It fills and feeds the eye everywhere with its fascinating works and ways. It cuts a blue pathway to the shadowed roots of the hills; it presents a foreground and mirror to the stately cliffs above; it becomes a bed of blue in which an emerald isle may float and dream; it is a nether sky in which the ocean birds swim and dive.

We are sitting on a hill-top in Yell, an island which is in bad odour among writers on Shetland. It has certainly got a bad name, but, for all that, it will take a lot of hanging. One writer says the word means *barren*, and is therefore most fitting and appropriate. But the complacent ignoramus gives us no hint of the derivation. It looks as if he keeps his etymological dictionary on that surface shelf of his mind which is labelled imagination. The name is said to be derived from an old Norse word "Yala," signifying health, and this is at least more probable, for, barren though it be, it is certainly a healthy island. It may also be well in this connection to warn all witty persons that already every possible outrage in the shape of pun or joke has been committed upon the name; but alas! none of the offenders have yet been brought to justice. A reward of one hundred pounds offered in the press for a really

O

new specimen might entrap the next criminal, while the
money itself would be absolutely safe. To show intending competitors to what level they must attain, I may
quote the best example of success in the past. There
is a parish on the mainland called Brae; and the story
goes that two young clergymen were sent north by the
same steamer—the one to *Brae* and the other to *Yell* in
the exercise of their office! Anything which falls short
of that standard of excellence must be condemned.

For myself, I have many pleasing memories of Yell.
In it I learnt more of the people of Shetland—their
character, circumstances, and manners—than anywhere
else in the islands. Allow me only a few words upon
their homes. A Shetland township consists of from five
or six to ten or twelve families—sometimes even more.
Their houses and cultivated land are enclosed by a turf
dyke not less than six feet high—the common protection
and boundary of the settlement. Outside, the sheep and
cattle all graze upon the *scathold* or common; inside,
the cultivated ground is commonly divided on the *run-
rig* system, that is to say, the first ridge belongs to
one family, the next to another, the next again to a
third, or in other cases they are held alternately by
two tenants. The natives look to the sea to provide
them daily food and oil for light, to the in-field for
bread and the sustenance of beast and fowl, and to the
out-field for pasture and fuel. The houses are in general
built of stone and fairly comfortable, but too many of
them are homes in which "nature is cook, and necessity
caterer." The Shetlanders rarely indulge in fresh ani-

mal food, and yet more rarely in luxuries, with the exception of tobacco. As to the interior, the houses closely resemble those of Lewis, but they are cleaner, more roomy, and more airy. In one particular there is a notable difference. In many Shetland houses the "but" end contains not only the family, but also the live stock of the farm with the exception of cattle and horses. Sheep and calves mingle with the children; the poultry bob about everywhere picking what they can find; the young pigs lie sleeping among the ashes around the central fire. All these creatures have in not a few cases the free run of this part of the premises; they have obtained burgess tickets for the "but" end of the dwelling.

By the way, some of the Shetland breed of pigs are most uncouth and repulsive-looking, being small, long-nosed, and covered with bristles almost like those of a hedgehog. Regarding these, a story is told which, *si non è vero, è ben trovato.* A Shetland vessel carrying a large number of pigs to the London market was wrecked off the Yorkshire coast, and two of the carcases were washed ashore. Never before had the natives beheld such creatures, and many conjectures were afloat as to their nature, name, and genus. At last they came under the skilled eye of the curator of a local museum. After due examination, he pronounced them to be marine monsters of a rare and remarkable type; and proved the sincerity of his opinion by buying them, stuffing them, and giving them a place among his treasures and curiosities of natural history.

Looking from Clothan Hill toward the south, there lies over some moorland ridges the bay of Hamnavoe, an excellent and almost land-locked place of anchorage. Several incidents of a varied kind are among my memories of that arm of the sea. On one occasion a party of young men, seven in number, of whom I was one, sailed into Hamnavoe about sunset and dropped anchor for the night. Our yacht, which we shall call the *Ruby*, had had a rattling run from Lerwick of less than four hours —the mainsail reefed, and the water swishing in through the lee scuppers. After some visits on shore we dropped below for the night, and, after supper and a smoke, prepared for rest. Meanwhile the wind, which had been high all day, rose into a moderate gale, and millions of heavy rain drops hissed and pattered on the deck above our heads. Being the party chiefly responsible for the cruise, I had many things to occupy my thoughts and could not drop into sleep. About midnight I thought I heard a cry as of a human voice. Listening intently I at length caught in a lull of the wind the words, " *Ruby* a-hoy ! " Knowing that two of our party were sleeping ashore, and fearing that something was wrong with them, I sprang up, and rapidly drew on some clothing. On reaching the slippery deck, the cry came again through the wind and rain, " *Ruby* a-hoy ! " " Aye, aye," I shouted in reply, " what do you want ? " By this time I had discovered that the voice came not from shore, but from a schooner-yacht which had crept into the voe at a late hour and anchored at no great distance from us. The cause of their distress was soon told.

"Our boat's gone ; the painter broke, and she's ashore somewhere among the rocks. Can you help us ?" Well, it was neither a pleasant nor a very safe enterprise on a dark stormy night, but I called up one of the men from the forecastle, and we determined to do what we could. Dropping into our own boat and shoving her off, we pulled near to the schooner, and then allowed ourselves to drift down upon the shore where the waves were spending themselves in very bad temper upon the rocks. The sea was not really high, for no wind can raise great rollers across a narrow bay ; but still it was ticklish work to drift in among the broken water after the truant boat. We found it at last, and having secured it with difficulty, towed it away in triumph, the only cost to ourselves being two or three nasty bumps upon the rocks, and a pretty considerable wetting. The party on the schooner were, I have no doubt, glad to get back their boat, but I am sorry to say I can remember no vote of thanks. The sailor and I had no chance of presenting our little bill for what we had done, for when we came on deck next morning the schooner was gone, and had not even left a P. P. C. card behind her. Is not this an ungrateful world ?

After a storm, a calm ; so it proved next morning. A more lovely inspiriting dawn I have seldom known. Summer had evidently set in, as Horace Walpole once said, "with its usual severity." Before breakfast some of our party went ashore as usual for milk, butter, and eggs, while others, if not all the rest, had a refreshing plunge overboard. On this particular morning, one of our company, a student, who could not swim, resolved to have a bath like his neighbours. Accordingly he tied a rope round his naked waist, and gave his comrades the other end to hold. Of course they promised not to betray him. Then he sprang from the gangway, not head foremost, but on his feet, as if taking a long leap at some athletic gathering. Down—down—down he sank, his head last covered by the in-curling waters, while the rope went whirring over the bulwarks, as if an anchor was at the end of it. How deep he went neither he nor anybody else can tell, for we forgot to measure the rope ; but "it's a long lane that has no turning." Of course he came up again in due time, and shook his dripping head. For a moment—only a moment—he was speechless with wonder at what he had seen below, but at length he found voice enough to cry, " Haul me in ! Quick! Haul me in!" There was the ring of true sincerity in his words, so his friends responded to his appeal as well as laughter would allow them. His little escapade was an excellent sauce to breakfast both for him and us. Perhaps he sometimes thinks of it even in the Colonies.

Hamnavoe has frequently been the scene of a whale hunt. Never did the fiery cross rouse the Highland clans to greater fury of enthusiasm than does the cry of " Whales ! whales !" in a peaceful Shetland township. I have said *township;* I might have added " or congrega-tion ;" for the great shoals of whales are said to have a special preference for the Day of Rest as a fitting season for their sportive incursions into the voes. Not once or twice, but frequently, have sermons been cut short, and churches emptied in sixty seconds, by the electric contagious cry of "Whales! whales!" On one occasion a minister, either in Shetland or Orkney—I forget which— bitterly complained of his hearers, not because they rose and left their pews to take to their boats instead, but because they would not give him time to get down from the pulpit, that he and they might *start fair* in the race for the shore. About twenty-five years ago a shoal of whales came into Hamnavoe on the sacred Day, just before the hour of public worship. Not a man went home to doff his Sunday clothes, and neither would they, even if attired in the richest of court costume. In ten minutes every tub that could hold water was launched and manned, and even those who had to run round to the opposite side of the voe for their boats soon put off from shore and joined in the chase. Not having been a witness, I shall not attempt to describe the exciting details of the hunt. Suffice it to say, that for a time the cordon of boats across the mouth of the voe, using every means of terror, vocal and mechanical, drove the whales inward, until some of them were almost ashore upon the beach. Then the finny monsters seemed all at once to realise their danger, and a panic set in. Lashing the waves in their fury, they charged wildly in amongst the boats, capsizing some, half-swamping others, and in a frantic stampede spread out fan-like into the open sea, and were gone. When the men, wet, weary, and dejected, returned home, there were some who said, "Served them right," and looked upon the escape of the whales as a providential rebuke for the abuse of the Day of Rest.

Now comes the point of special interest. One elder of the kirk, a man of excellent character, was among the raiders, and was taken to task for his share in the proceedings. His defence before the minister and kirk-session was very remarkable in its way. If true, it was, to say the least, peculiar; if not true, it was ingenious. He was ready for church when the Fiery Cross cry reached his ears. He saw the whales sporting in the voe, and the rush of men and women to the shore. His own boat was down upon the beach, and he went to secure it, lest some one who had no right to do so might launch and use it. When he arrived on the spot his worst suspicions were realised. His boat had already been drawn down to the water's edge, and her stern was actually afloat. What could he do but spring in, and warn off those who were to use his property for an unlawful purpose? Unfortunately the wicked men whose hands were on the gunwale did not see it in that light, so no sooner was the elder in his boat than they shoved her off, and took him with them to the chase. Whether he lay down, sullen and vengeful, in the bottom of the boat and groaned the time away over his misfortune, I cannot say; indeed, I have heard some whispers to the contrary. What the upshot was I really do not remember, but his action forcibly reminds me of a notable name in British history. When Charles the Second came to Scotland, he signed the Solemn League and Covenant. To many, knowing what

manner of man he was, this must have seemed a strange
act on his part. The explanation has been neatly put
in brief words. " They compelled him to do it volun-
tarily." If the elder had known this little episode in
Scottish history, he might have used it as a defence or
excuse. This much is certain, that if it amounted to any
palliation in the case of the king, it would surely have
been more than sufficient in the case of the fisherman.

Let me present one picture more e'er we descend from
the Hill of Clothan. Most of you have, I daresay,
heard of a June midnight in Shetland. One such at
least I have spent on this height, and several others in
open boats at sea. If anywhere in this United Kingdom
midnight is truly a " witching " hour, it must be in the
north isles of Shetland.

> " Here the light of evening lies
> Longer than in summer skies."

So I certainly found it on the Hill of Clothan. When I
reached my point of observation—the heap of stones on
this heathery brow—the last faint streaks of gold were
fading out of the northern hills of the mainland. The
purple rays of the sun grew like the petals of a flower
out of the far Atlantic, and then spread outwards and
upwards like a fan over the western sky. Thin fleecy
banks of cloud edged with orange and yellow lay here
and there across the heavens ; and beneath them, in the
far north-west, the great orb rolled himself over the horizon and dropped out of sight. But delicate tints, like
tender memories of some loved one departed, yet lingered
in the sky and slowly glided over the northern sea,

which caught their colours on its face. On and on, even to and beyond the midnight hour, every headland and island and voe retained their distinct outline and familiar features. They were far less obscured than I had more than once seen them on a dark day of storm. About midnight the deeper colours melted imperceptibly into lighter shades, and at length the sun rose again, now in the far north-east, under a fresh canopy of yellow and gold. One had not fully realised his absence till he began to creep back over the shoulder of the world and look you in the face again. He had lain down as it were for a brief rest, and now he greeted us again after a fresh bath in the Arctic seas.

The parish of Hillswick, on the north-west of the Mainland, contains scenery of quite peculiar interest. Its ragged and contorted coast-line is exposed to the unbroken force and fury of the Atlantic billows, and Neptune has carved the rocks into many a weird and wanton form. Some of these our yacht party were anxious to see, so we left the *Ruby* at Ollaberry one morning, and trudged over hill and moor to Hillswick. On the way out to the more distant points of the coast, we had striking views of cliffs whose heads seemed to nod over the waters, picturesque stacks out at sea like a group of fishing boats with their brown sails hanging idly in a calm, and rocky islands pierced with tall arches, like great sea-elephants stooping to drink, and unable to lift their heads again. By and by we came to a solitary enclosed churchyard, and wandered among the tombstones in search of anything interesting or curious.

Our quest was not in vain, for we found the following epitaph :—

"DONALD ROBERTSON,

Born 1st January 1785 ; died 4th June 1848.

Aged 63 years.

He was a quiet peaceable man, and, to all appearance, a good Christian. His death was very much regretted, which was caused by the stupidity of Laurence Tulloch, of Clothester, who sold him nitre instead of Epsom salts, by which he was killed in the space of three hours after taking of it."

Who the cultivated and considerate writer of the inscription was, I cannot tell ; tradition ascribes it to the parish minister. This, however, is, I believe, true and well known, that ere very long the unfortunate Laurence was obliged to flee from the islands and hide himself in the shadows of Edinburgh.

From the graveyard we had still a long and stiff walk to the cliffs we wished to see. Some of our company had already dropped off, wishing us *bon voyage*, and engaging to have all ready for us on board the yacht when we returned. Acting on the Bulgarian proverb that a shower cannot hurt him who is wet to the skin, the rest of us scorned our fatigue, and resolved to see all we could. I ventured, having been there before, to promise my comrades that they should not be disappointed. At length we reached a table-land of soft rich grass, the further edge of which dropped in wild walls of rock sheer down into the sea. Here indeed were great wonders of nature.

Almost ere we were aware, we came upon the edge of the Holes of Scraada. These are immense cavernous pits, perhaps one hundred feet deep from the grassy verge above

to the level of the restless water below. They are connected with the ocean by means of a long black tunnel,
for the front of the cliffs is some 300 yards away. It is
said that a boat has passed through from the sea outside into the great pit in front of us, but it scarcely
seems possible. The bottom of one of these awful holes
is half beach and half water; in the other only water
and no beach is to be seen. In storms they are filled
with tossing, raging foam, and the spray rises in pillars
of cloud above the surrounding grass.

Still further along the green plateau above the cliffs, a
still more wonderful sight may be witnessed. It is called
the Grind (or Gateway) of the Navir, but I have been
unable to discover the origin or meaning of the latter
word. Has it anything to do with the Latin *navis*, a ship,
or with the termination of Scandin*avia*? Here the ocean
waves have burst an entrance through the cliffs from
without, and delight, when tide and wind are high, to
rush in and out between the jaws of rock. The door-
posts of this gateway are immense masses of unyielding
porphyry. If ever there was a lintel over their heads it
has long ago been torn away and tossed in fragments far
in upon the land. In times of wild western tempest the
waves lift from the bed of the sea and from its shore
great masses of rock—sometimes six, eight, and ten tons
in weight—and hurl them like pebbles through the raging Grind on to the plateau behind. Probably no human
eye ever saw this deed done, for no one dare approach the
spot at such times; but the evidences of its reality and
frequency are plain enough. The threshold of the Grind

is fairly level, but behind there are enormous boulders and stones piled one above another over a wide area—like the *débris* of one of Nature's great quarries, out of which were built the giant cliffs of Foula and Noss and the Skaw of Unst. Many a man would give almost anything if he could safely stand just inside the gateway in a storm, and behold the ocean in the very wantonness of conscious power thus sporting with its toys. For those who can be impressed with figures, I may add that many of these huge cubical masses have been tossed inland 180 feet; and it has been estimated by the highest authorities that the pressure of the waves at the Grind must often be not less than 6000 lbs. on the square foot.

Near by these striking objects, there is yet another worthy of notice. Beneath one of these lofty cliffs the waves rush into a deep cavern, whose recesses are hidden far out of sight. At its inner end it must be curved upward, for it opens out on the face of the cliff again like the mouth of a cannon, and so the *Cannon* it is called. From this singular freak and phenomenon of Nature comes a most striking result. In high westerly gales, when immense billows roll inward from the ocean, they dash into the cave and fill to the very full its every recess. Then the pressure from without forces the water upward, and from the Cannon mouth it bursts out at intervals as with the speed of lightning and the boom of a thunder peal. All around this Hillswick coast—the scenery of which is often fantastic and as often sublime, it may well be said—

"The everlasting waters flow,
And round the precipices vast
Dance to the music of the blast."

Many of my readers may desire to know something of
the Shetland dialect. I have already spoken of it as a
form of broad Scotch with a considerable sprinkling of
Norse words and idioms. As spoken by the islanders
generally, it is sweet, simple, almost tender; yet it is
capable of expressing the most powerful emotions. The
two features which first and most strike a stranger are
the almost entire absence of the *th* sound, for which the
letter *d* or *dh* is always substituted, and the use of the
singular pronoun *du* and *de* (or rather *dhu* and *dhe*) for
the plural *you* and *ye*. In this respect their speech resembles that of the Society of Friends. Many English
words are also cut short or softened so much that
strangers with difficulty recognise them at all. Here I
had intended to make an attempt to reproduce some
scraps of conversation between natives and myself, but I
have found a safer and more excellent way. At Fethaland or Feidaland, the extreme northern point of the
Mainland, there is a summer fishing station, to which
boats resort in large numbers from both sides of Yell
Sound. There are two kinds of fishing recognised in
Shetland. If it be carried on in small boats near
shore, it is called the *Eela*, referring probably to the *isles*
round about which it is prosecuted. The other is the
"Haaf" fishing, when the men go in large six-oared
boats far out to sea, and generally remain out two nights
at least at a time. I do not know the origin of the

name. Well, I have before me a description of a voyage
to the Haaf fishing as given by a fisherman at Fethaland,
and I cannot do better than embody it here. I leave
the spelling almost untouched, but have ventured to
insert some explanatory words in parenthesis.

"Mony a foul dae hae I seen at da Haaf, but I tink
Martanabullimas dae fearn year (year before last) wis ta
warst dae I ever saw. He wis a bonny morning, but a
grit lift (great swell) i' da sea, an' a hantle o' brak itil
'im. Sae I sed ta wir men, 'We hae a guid nebert
(quantity) o' bait ; he's bonny wadder (weather), an' I
tink we'll try da deep watter.' Sae we gat wir tows an'
cappiestanes (sinkers) itida (into the) boat, an' we set aff,
an' we rowed oot upon him (*i.e.,* the sea) till we sank
da laigh land, an' dan (then) we began an' led fram
(seaward), an' whin we cuist (cast) wir ooter bow (buoy)
deel a stane o' Shetland cood we see incep (except) da
tap o' Roünis Hill an' da Pobies o' Unst. Noo he
begood (it began) ta gro (blow hard) frae da sud-
aest, sae whan we'd sitten a peerie (little) while, we
tuik wir bow an' begood ta hail an' haith ! afore
we gat in ae packie o' tows (one bundle of lines)
fower men cood dü nae mair ir keep hir ida (in the)
kaib (thowl). We gat twa ir tree fish frae dat, an' at
last sic a grit weight cam' upuda (upon the) line dat it
tuik a' mi strent ta hail (all my strength to haul), an'
whin it cam' tida wyle (gunwale) what wis it bit a grit
devil o' a skate. Sae I sed ta Tammie, 'Cut hir awa',
wha's gawn ta row in onder hir wi' sic a dae.' Sae he
tuik da skünie (knife) an's needed (cut) da tome (small

line with hook). An' at last we gat in wir tows an' haith! we wir gotten a braw puckle o' fish. 'Noo,' says I, 'boys, i' Gude's name, fit ta mast an' swift ta sail, da aest tide is rinnin', an' we'll sail wast-an'-be sooth ipun him.' Sae I gaed ida starn, an' jüist as we led till ta sail, he med a watter aff o' da fore kaib, an' whin 'e brook (broke), he tuik Heckie aff o' da skair taft (after seat) an' led 'im ida shott (stern). Dan I cried ta Gibbie, 'for Gudesake strik (strike) ta heid oot o' da drink kig an' owse (bale) de boat,' for da watter wis up ta wir fastabaands (cross-beams); bit wi' Gude's help we gat hir toomed afore anider watter cam'. Whin da aest tide wis rin aff, I says, 'Boys, we'll tak' down ta sail an' we'll row in ipun him,' an' sae we did, an' whin ta wast tide med, we gae sail ageen, an we ran aest ipun him, an' haith! we lay ipa Vaalafield in Unst, an' we vrocht on rowin' an' sailin' till, by Gude's providence, we gat ta wir ain banks aboot aucht o'clock at nicht. Oh, man, dat wis a foul dae."

It has always been understood in Shetland that the fairies—the "guid folk"—show more regard to the wishes of some human beings than others. When one whom they are wont to obey desires to send them away home, he uses this most interesting formula—

" Da twal, da twal aposels,
  Da eleven, da eleven evengelists,
  Da ten, da ten commanders,
  Da nine da brazen sheeners,
  Da eicht da holy waters,
  Da seven starns i' da heavens,
  Da six creation mornins,

Da five da tumblers o' my bools,
Da four da gospel makers,
Da tree triddle trivers,
Da twa lily-white boys dat clothe demsells in green, boys ;
Da ane, da ane, dat walks alon, an' now ye'se a' gang hame, boys."

Now I have found, as much to my surprise as to my regret, that many Shetland people have scarcely heard of any such lines, and—still more strange—I can get no one to interpret them all. Twelve apostles ; eleven evangelists ; ten commandments : so far, all is plain sailing. Nine brazen sheeners ; lamps, I suppose, but what or where they were, I cannot guess. Eight holy waters ; perhaps eight sacred rivers, but if so, what are they ? The next two are evident, seven stars—the Pleiades ; and six mornings of creation. Number five is a complete mystery, and will, I fear, remain so. The four are Matthew, Mark, Luke, and John. The three gave me much trouble, but through aid from a friend well acquainted with Norse, I think I have got the key. Triddle may mean treadle, the part of a loom wrought by the feet. Then there is a Norwegian word *trive* or *triver*, to drive. Putting these two together, the expression seems to point to the Fates—Clotho, Lachesis, and Atropos—weaving the web of human destiny. The remaining lines are plain enough. I remember the police in a German university town chanting similar lines through the various watches of the night. The Shetlander sometimes uttered his word of command to the fairies in much briefer language, such as—

" Skeet howe hame, guid folk,"

P

that is, "slide quickly home, good folk." What a pity they are so few in number, or so rarely seen,

> "The joyous nymphs and light-foot fairies,
>   Which thither came to hear their music sweet,
> And to the measure of their melodies,
>   Did learn to move their nimble-shifting feet."

A few days before leaving Lerwick on the occasion of my last visit, an advertisement of a pleasure excursion caught my eye and took my fancy. The North Isles steamer, the *Earl of Zetland*, was to make a special run to Sumburgh Head and Fitful Head, which, with the fine bay of Quendal between them, form the double southern extremity of the Shetland Islands. Having time and leisure I resolved to take advantage of the opportunity for a day's "outing." There were, I should fancy, about two hundred on board—a medley company of all ranks and classes. As is invariably the case on such occasions, there were several clergymen in the number, disguised in suits of russet and grey, and therefore less threatening than they often are to the public in general. It is matter of common experience that, if you wish to prevent overcrowding in a railway carriage, all you have got to do is to show a baby or a white necktie at the window—the former as small as you like, the latter the larger the better. We had also at least one limb of the law, a number which is decidedly below the general average in human society, for legal gentlemen have abounded, one might almost say like birds of prey, in all ages. You remember how on one occasion Pope Innocent claimed from the Marquis of Carpio a levy of

30,000 swine. The marquis could not supply so large
a number, but told the Pope that instead of these useful
animals he was willing to put 30,000 lawyers at his
service. As to whether Innocent was innocent enough
to accept the alternative tribute, history is silent. Then
we had a journalist on board, who was, of course, "takin'
notes," and has, I believe, printed them since that time.
He was a jolly specimen of the cynical, critical class,
one of whose functions it is, like servants, to "brush the
dust out of gentlemen's clothes." On the upper deck
we had a fair sprinkling of ladies, married and un-
married alike. Among the latter, it is almost needless
to say, there were one or two spinsters, of strong convictions and stationary age. Some recollections of past
history led me to the conclusion that they had come
into the world by bad luck a century later than their
proper epoch. It flashed across my memory that,
according to thoroughly reliable records, a female
parliament was proposed or established in Edinburgh
more than a hundred years ago. Whether it still exists
or no, I cannot tell; but rumour says that there are
persons, practices, and proceedings in and about the
Parliament House to this day which minister to the
impression that some of the honourable members, now
advancing in years, still linger within the precincts.
It is, however, with the past that we have here to do.
Among other measures annually introduced, or proposed
to be introduced, into the said parliament was, of course,
a budget. It had a preamble, and in that preamble its
object was defined to be, " To raise the necessary supplies

of husbands throughout the country." I only mention this because I am sure that one, at least, of our company on board the *Earl of Zetland* would, if financial minister at the time, have made a speech on that subject compared with which Mr Gladstone's finest efforts would seem poor indeed.

On the lower deck there was evidently quite as great a variety as on the upper deck and bridge ; and in that region, before our voyage came to an end, everybody, including the crew, seemed to know everybody else, and the utmost harmony prevailed.

Steaming out by the southern strait of Bressay Sound, we skirted the rugged promontory of the Knab, of which a curious old story may be told. Paul Jones, the celebrated pirate, once approached this spot in his vessel with the amiable intention of sacking the town of Lerwick. But as they drew near, he and his crew observed that the crest of the Knab was covered with figures in brilliant scarlet. Who could these be, thought they, but a few stragglers from a garrison of red coats, sent thither by the Government for the protection of the town ? What if he had known his error ? They were only groups of Shetland women arrayed in gorgeous petticoats of the warlike hue ! That interesting discovery, as it might have been, he did not make. On the contrary, nearer approach only confirmed his suspicions, and ere long he turned his ship's head, and fled the coast with all convenient speed.

After an hour's sail we passed the island of Mousa, with its lofty circular Broch or castle, one remnant and evidence of the very early Pictish occupation of these islands. Shetland possesses many such Brochs or their remains, but of all these Mousa is the most perfect, and therefore the most valuable in the eyes of the antiquary. That gentleman, rarer surely than he once was, or less distinctive in appearance and habits, is not a bad sort of fellow after all, when you come to know him well. How he has been lashed alike in prose and poetry let two extracts show. Pope tells all of them who care to listen that they are

> "Foes to all living work except your own,
> And advocates for folly dead and gone."

Even more severe are the words of Samuel Butler, who says, " He despises the present age as an innovation, and slights the future ; but has a great value for that which is past and gone, like the madman who fell in love with Cleopatra." The truth is that the work of the antiquary is to himself an innocent and great delight, and may prove in many directions of immense value to his fellow-men. In most cases all that he needs to make him an agreeable and useful member of society is to convince him that Dr Chalmers was right in his declaration, "Truly speaking, we are the fathers ; the ancients are the children."

By the time we were abreast of Mousa, we should have been able to see Sumburgh Head, but, alas for the success of our expedition! down came a thick mist over land and sea alike. We reached with some difficulty and risk the opening of Grutness Voe—about three miles short of the famous promontory, and into it we slowly crept and dropped anchor. The captain told us he dare not go any further in such a fog, so he landed the whole company to wander where they pleased, but charged us all to return to the vessel not a moment later than six o'clock.

The party, of which I formed one, visited first the ruins of Jarl's Hof, famed as the residence of the "Pirate," and thence, after a stiff walk, the lighthouse of Sumburgh Head. From the latter great elevation we gazed down as well as the mist would allow over the stern cliffs and fearsome goes—those narrow gullies of rock in which the waves crawl and swirl—which surround the headland. Peering over the dizzy heights, it was a scene to recall the words of Gloster—

> " The murmuring surge
> That on the unnumber'd idle pebbles chafes
> Cannot be heard so high ; I'll look no more
> Lest my brain turn, and the deficient sight
> Topple down headlong."

Right in front of the rocks we could hear to right and left, as well as immediately before us, the murmuring roar of the tide in the dreaded " Roost" of Sumburgh, so happily chosen by the great wizard Scott as the scene of the wreck of the " Pirate." There the Gulf Stream, setting eastward towards Norway, and finding the long Mainland of Shetland an obstruction in the way, sweeps at the rate of 12 or 14 miles an hour round the headland—rushing, curling, leaping, diving—ever restless, ever roaring—a wonder by day and a terror by night.

When we regathered on board the steamer at the
appointed hour, the mist had "lifted" just a little, and
the captain thought he might venture out in the hope
that the sky might be clearer over the open sea. It was
a bold venture, but, alas! a vain hope. Scarcely had
we cleared the voe of Grutness than the mist fell down
denser than ever. We could not be safe anywhere near
so wild and rocky a coast, seeing that we could not see
even a faint outline of anything in the shape of land.
Treacherous currents might sweep us away in any direction in a very brief space of time. Accordingly, it was
not long before the captain turned the ship's head due
east and gave the command, "Full speed ahead." Had
they understood anything at all, not a few on board
might have supposed that they were off on a jaunt to
Norway. Many will at once recall the remarkable
adventure of the old woman a few years ago who, helpless and alone, yet safely after all, was drifted in a sloop
from Shetland to one of the fiords of the Norsemen. To
some of us, however, the captain had confided the comforting secret that he meant to steam straight east for
at least two hours until well clear of the land, and then let
the vessel roll about in the sea as she pleased for the night.
This was a cheering prospect, and it was fully realised.

In a short time the hatches were removed, and the
hold down in front of the bridge was transformed into
a ballroom. At first there was a certain shyness on the
part of the young ladies. By way of breaking the ice,
one or two couples of the sterner sex opened the dance
to the screeching and scraping of a fiddle. The said

instrument, I regret to say, was not a Straduarius. Still, it served its purpose for want of a better; and ere long men and maidens many, with vigorous *hochs* and *hoochs*, twisted and whirled in the giddy dance, while the spectators below and others looking over the rim of the hatches supplied a further accompaniment of gabble and laughter. For a time we watched the proceedings from the bridge with much interest and amusement, but I confess there came a gradual but decided change of feeling. The interest gave place to indifference, that indifference to annoyance, that annoyance to irritation, and that irritation to something on the very borderland of resentment.

There were, if I remember aright, only four berths in the dingy, stuffy cabin, so that the ladies could not seek refuge either in retirement or sleep. Besides, there were at least thirty or forty persons to ballot for the places, even if they had been a little more attractive than they were. Supper might have been a relief or an interlude, but, alas! the steward's pantry had long since been despoiled of everything except dishes and glasses. These, however useful on a table, are generally considered unsuitable for human food. There was nothing to drink, for even the fresh water was all gone, and nothing to eat, so that the cook could not, even if so inclined, make our meat our misery. Despite all this, we were wonderfully happy on the bridge, and might have been almost perfectly so, but for the racket and noise below, and especially the everlasting squeak, squeak, squeak, squeak, of the wretched, waspish fiddle, out of which evidently only one pretence of a tune could be produced. I also confess that more than once I began to question whether dancing really is after all "the poetry of motion."

Those long midnight hours were, without doubt, a fitting season to moralize. We had two great consolations. One of these, the lesser, was the fact that, despite the fog, the sea was smooth, the air mellow, and the wind far away. Only our outer garments were dusted over with tiny globules out of the mist, and the sleeping vessel at times turned uneasily in its bed, as people often do when away from home.

Our other comfort lay, as you have doubtless guessed already, in the society of the ladies. Here of course I dare not enter into particulars, for I was not a Benedict, though alone for the time being; but I am sure we on the bridge, not less than our brethren and sisters in the hold, were confirmed in the belief that neither sex can do without the other. Poetry—always a faithful interpreter of human life and feeling—has fully recognised this fact. Think, too, how impartial she is, giving due weight to both sides of the question! We all remember Campbell's lines,

> "Without the smile from partial beauty won,
> Oh, what were man! A world without a sun!"

That is one side of the picture; now, look at the other—

> "Take man from *woman*—all that she can show
> Of her own proper, is nought else but *wo!*"

We found the nice balance of these two companion

truths sweetly realised on the bridge of the *Earl of Zetland*, not less than twenty miles to the east of the Shetland Islands.

When morning dawned we crept cautiously westward again, and by-and-by fell in with a fishing boat. We hailed the crew, and asked where we were. They told us we were just off the Island of Mousa. Turning our ship's head to the northward, we sailed straight for the Sound of Bressay, and landed at Lerwick just in time for a late breakfast. John Foster, in his journal, says, that all pleasure must be bought at the price of pain, and that the difference between false pleasure and true is just this : for the true, the price is paid before you enjoy it—for the false, after you enjoy it. In view of that nice distinction, I am at a loss whether to call that breakfast a true pleasure or a false, for we paid for it both *before* and *after* the enjoyment.

If my readers have found as much pleasure in perusing these " Scenes and Stories " of the Highlands and Islands of Scotland as I have had in writing them, my work shall not have been in vain.

TURNBULL AND SPEARS, PRINTERS, EDINBURGH.

www.ingramcontent.com/pod-product-compliance
Lightning Source LLC
Chambersburg PA
CBHW030355270326
41926CB00009B/1118